SAC Brat

A Personal Memoir

Don Evans

SAC Brat: A Personal Memoir

This memoir reflects the author's recollections and opinions.

Cover and interior photographs are from the author's family collection.

First Edition

979-8-9971993-0-2

Table of Contents

Acknowledgements

I am indebted to Dr. Frank "Mick" McKeown for his expertise and advice in the writing of this book. Mick is a graduate of the Department of Defense and State Department co-sponsorial National War College in Washington D.C. where he later served as the Deputy and Acting Chair of the Department of International Studies, one of the three major academic departments within the college. The National War college is the United States Government preeminent institution addressing grand strategy and the utilization of the national resources necessary to implement that strategy.

At Dr. McKeown's request I will not further review his impressive career responsibilities and awards while serving the defense establishment of our nation for over 50 years. I must site that on 10 May 2017, Dr. Mick McKeown was presented with the United States Air Force Exceptional Public Service Award, the highest citation the Chief of Staff of the Air Force is empowered to grant to a non-DOD civilian.

My son Saxon Rowdy Evans is a brilliant young man and at age 21 likely the youngest person to qualify as an Investment Advisor in Florida. He achieved his MBA at age 22 at the University of Florida. At age 32 he has surpassed my efforts in the financial realm. I thank him for his assistance with this book. I further thank him for accompanying me on so many research trips around the world. I doubt if I could have made it through Egypt, Sudan, Jordan, Israel, Truk Lagoon, Guadalcanal, China, Cambodia, India, Vietnam, Korea, Japan, Romania, Russia (Volgograd, Kursk, and Trans Siberia Railroad) and even the Wolf's Lair in eastern Poland without his help. Rowdy's grandfather Colonel Richard Evans would be proud of the honest, successful man Saxon has become.

Prologue: Four Dimensions of the Story

There will be four dimensions or fractals to this story. The first is the history of European domination of the world leading up to our time. The second is the experiences of a pilot named Colonel Richard Evans with particular emphasis on his military career. His life encompasses the later portion of European hegemony, a European Civil War and a struggle between the two victors of that war, or the Cold War. The third, and the source of the title, are the life observations of a child growing up on Strategic Air Command military bases in America during the later time. That life saw the likely peak of European progeny nation's power and the transition to a different world. The fourth covers the lessons learned and some conclusions about markets, the economy and their possible connection with each other and war.

PART ONE: THE WORLD THAT MADE THE WAR

Chapter 1: The Forge of Nations

Western Europe in the mid 1400's was a patchwork of small nations with weak central governments. The Great Golden Horde Mongol Empire was receding. The first level powers in the world were the Ottoman Empire, Mughal Empire (India), Golden Horde and China. The Franks or French were moving close to a unified nation the size of present-day Texas. Spain was gradually uniting by driving out the Moors and Portugal was becoming a nation. The British Isles were in the process of unification. Muscovy was moving to drive out the Golden Horde.

The Europeans were forced to travel through the Ottoman Empire to penetrate the Middle East and trade with India and China. This could only be established via overland caravans across Asia or shipping across the Mediterranean Sea, offloading ships, employing caravans across the Middle East, and loading back on ships. The journeys were very costly and dangerous. The tolls and tariffs were high.

The solution, as any historian knows, was to use ships to sail around Africa and eventually sail to the Americas and seek a passage through those continents to Asia. Prince Henry the Navigator of Portugal with Vasco da Gama developed the trade route around Africa and the profits were immense.

Scientists tell us that at present the greatest result of the modern Space Program was to incentivize new technologies to solve the problems of sending humans into space. These inventions not only helped in space but built tremendous civilian and military businesses. Building ships that could travel and navigate for months with crews from the Atlantic to Indian Ocean route was a revolutionary accomplishment and provided stimulus to the Portuguese economy.

The same force motivated the Spanish, followed by the English, French, Dutch, and Russians. Necessity is the mother of invention.

I recall growing up at Offutt Air Force Base, Nebraska and my father Colonel Richard Evans telling me the story of Glenn Cunningham.

Cunningham as a boy, had the job of turning on the kerosene heater in his school. One day his brother accidentally used gasoline as the heater's fuel. This resulted in an explosion which killed Cunningham's brother and badly burned Cunningham's toes. Several were burned off. The doctor wanted to amputate one of Cunningham's feet. Cunningham's family refused. While experiencing great pain, Glenn learned to walk again. The pain was so great that Cunningham was forced for years to run and not walk the long distance to school. The result was that Cunningham, as an adult, became the greatest runner of his time and nearly broke the four-minute mile. Bodybuilders understand that to build muscle they must tear it down. Muscles develop almost like scar tissue. The bodybuilders' motto is "no pain, no gain."

Colonel Evans told me of Demosthenes and his weak childhood voice. This great Greek leader and orator developed his vocal power as a child by placing pebbles in his mouth forcing him to speak more clearly. A legend is that Demosthenes ran along the beach and practiced yelling above the sound of the waves breaking on the shoreline. Another example I witnessed was Wilma Rudolph, the black Olympic Champion. She had polio as a child and was forced to wear a metal brace until age twelve, yet she later won three gold medals at the 1960 Olympics.

Psychiatrists describe how a person with a weakness or disability, often becomes stronger than the average due to overcompensation. The key is to confront the weakness and not run from it. This was a lesson taught to me as the child of a Strategic Air Command (SAC) officer. These children were affectionately known as SAC Brats. I would even say that the culture at SAC was to attack weakness, knowing that it brought excellence.

There is a predominant reason that small European nations could become world powers. It is simply an overcompensation. A weakness or problem is identified, and the nation is challenged. It can ignore the challenge and risk little, or the nation can attack the weakness. It then plays catch-up with often serendipitous discoveries benefiting the courageous nation. The result is greater power. Thus, the small European nations embarked on a colonial adventure for profit. They warred against each other, and this even made them stronger for war develops technology.

Nietzsche had the right idea when he said, "that which does not kill you makes you stronger."

Many Europeans were getting killed but their nations lived and their societies were learning and getting stronger and richer. Meanwhile the Ottoman Empire, India and China, comfortable in their position, fell technologically further behind.

The next most important factor was likely the unification of various European nations. Portugal and Spain were early to unify, and they were the first to embark on developing the Atlantic trade routes and to explore the unknown. France, England and the Dutch were late in the race but then overcompensated with the result that they took the lead at various times. The Germans, Italians, and non-European Japanese unified their states 300 years later. This was to cause great problems in the 20th century and the focus of Colonel Richard Evans' life and to a lesser extent his SAC Brat son.

Geography was another important factor in the success of Europeans. The two nations furthest west jutting into the Atlantic Ocean were Portugal and Spain. They enjoyed unblocking access to the Atlantic. While the Nordic Europeans Norway and Denmark while first to cross the Atlantic, were geographically hindered by the British Isles. The French and British enjoyed direct access to the Atlantic.

The Dutch enjoyed reasonable access via the English Channel but were partially blocked by Britain. Russia was blocked by the Baltic and Black Sea nations from expanding into the Atlantic. The result was Russian expansion across the steppes of Eurasia in reverse of the Mongol conquests before.

Great Britain, an island nation, had the most ideal geography. It had unblocked access to the Atlantic and like an ancient castle, a large moat of water making invasion extremely difficult. The United States possesses that great advantage in our time. The threat to British security was the unification of Europe under one power. This would allow that nation to focus all its resources on building a naval force to conquer Britain. The Dutch canal system provided a water barrier like Britain but on a less effective scale.

Which factor made Great Britian great-was it the nature of its people or it geographic position?

France had the finest farmland in Europe which resulted in a great advantage in domestic population versus the other European powers. Lacking an ocean moat, France was forced to divide its military resources between its army and navy.

Early European explorations tended to flow at a similar latitude to the mother country. This was likely due to a comfort factor and that their technology was best in a similar climate. The northern Europeans sought out regions they were used to. That is in the northern part of America. These were not regions ideal for large empires. The Portuguese and Spanish were more comfortable in an almost tropical climate, and they tended to settle in those regions. The French and British enjoyed access to the Atlantic, unblocked by any other power, and to regions of similar climate.

From the time of Columbus to the 20th Century the leading colonial powers were likely in this order:

- **1400s**: Portugal, Spain
- **1500s**: Spain, Portugal, Dutch, French, British
- **1600s**: Spain, Dutch, French, British, Portuguese
- **1700s**: Great Britain, French, Dutch, Spanish, Portuguese
- **1800s**: Great Britain, French, Dutch, Belgian, German, United States, Japanese, Spanish, Italian, Portuguese
- **1900s**: First half Britain, France, Japanese, Dutch, Belgian, United States, Spanish, Italian, Portuguese. Second half Soviet Union and United States (military bases)
- **2000s**: Colonial Power as defined by military bases around the world. United States.

Note how various nations dominated, became too complacent, and were then replaced by more dynamic people. This process evolved ultimately in wars between mainly European powers for control. For example, the mighty Portuguese Empire was reduced by the Dutch Empire which was reduced by the British Empire. After World War II the U. S. took over control of most of the British Empire. The wars were the test of geography, cyclic stage of decay in the empires, resources, and technologies of the systems. The strongest survived just as in the animal kingdom.

We can conclude that nations rise because of the willingness of their people to sacrifice and overcompensate themselves to gain advantage. They lose advantage relative to other powers due to their very success which weakens the nations morally and reduces the nation's willingness to sacrifice. The expression "shirt sleeve to shirt sleeve in three generations" tells the same story in a family or personal way. The grandparents make sacrifices and build success. Their children are not as driven but with greater advantage, and some drive push success forward. The grandchild has advantages but no pressure to be successful so dynastic success weakens. I believe this is true in nature and all areas of competition including families, sport teams, and nations.

There was an awareness of the tendency of the successful to get lazy and to rot over time in the Strategic Air Command (SAC) ethos led by General Curtis LeMay. LeMay wanted to avoid an atomic Pearl Harbor, knowing that a successful First Strike on the United States might end the war in minutes. General LeMay tried to always keep SAC on a war footing. A certain percentage of pilots were always on alert. Their children or the SAC Brats were always aware of this environment. These children knew they resided on a target. LeMay took this policy so far that he organized fake invasions of the bases to test the defenses and reactions of the troops guarding the bases.

The greatest factor in European success was the Industrial Revolution. This was encouraged by European overcompensation and the need for technological innovation. The sweet spot in the world was Great Britain. The textile industry was first to feel the effects of loom development and the use of water power to drive the machines. In a way, the Industrial Revolution was brought on by the T-shirt. England became the clothing manufacturer for the world. Soon coal and the steam engine greatly improved in the efficiency of the British textile industry. Britain sat on a mountain of coal. Coal was discovered in France, Northern Italy, Japan, and later importantly in Silesia and the Ruhr in Germany, the Donbas in Russia, and the United States. It was just the beginning.

The Industrial Revolution brought on by European competition spawned huge changes in all sectors of human life as science and machines dominated. New farming techniques and medicine greatly increased human survivability and life spans. The result was that by 1900 white Europeans ruled most of the world and represented around 35% of the earth's population. It was at this time that my great grandmother, who faced starvation in Norway, immigrated to find a better life in America.

A factor that speeded up colonialization was Eurasian disease. Eurasians over centuries had built up a decent level of immunity to smallpox, measles and the common cold. In some regions of the Americas which lacked immunity, it is estimated that 90% of the populations were destroyed due to exposure to these diseases.

The more feudalistic societies like Spain and Portugal were likely at a disadvantage to the relatively capitalistic British, Dutch and French. This disadvantage likely negatively affected their colonies in America. The more individualistic economies of Britain and particularly America spawned an almost Cincinnatus character. The minuteman farmer who when called to war put down his plough share for a sword or a musket. The feudalistic societies in Africa and South America were heavily slave based and lacked this ready-made, self-interested militia.

Chapter 2: A Place in the Sun

"All we want is a place in the sun." Kaiser Wilhelm II, 1901

Prior to American Admiral Perry's visit to Japan in the mid 1800's, trade with that nation was highly restricted. The United States and Britain practically forced at gunpoint the opening of the Japanese market. The Japanese leadership could see the technological superiority of the Western Nations and realized that if Japan did not unify and industrialize it would be a colony of some European based country.

In a remarkable achievement Japan unified and industrialized by 1900. As Japanese industrialization increased Japanese power, Japan embarked on colonial wars winning territory in Korea and Taiwan, At the turn of the century, Japan acquired Manchuria and defeated the partially industrialized Russians in the 1905 war.

The Japanese greatly admired the British model of success. Both nations were islands off the coast of Eurasia. This allowed Japan like England to focus on her navy. Many early Japanese warships were built by the British in English shipyards.

When World War I broke out in Europe, Japan took advantage of German Asian weakness and captured the German Caroline Islands in the central Pacific. Japanese warships even assisted in transporting Australian troops to Egypt to participate in the Gallipoli landings.

Japan lacked resources in its home waters, thus continued its policy of enlarging its colonial possessions. Of particular interest to the Japanese was the oil controlled by the Dutch in the East Indies.

Italy, once the center of the Roman Empire, was a fragmented nation during the first half of the Nineteenth Century. Pope Pius IX controlled large amounts of the peninsula. Other major players were the Austrians and French. After a series of wars Italy became a unified nation around 1865 with its capital in Rome. The Pope's worldly territory was reduced to the small Vatican City.

Like the Japanese, the Italians industrialized and embarked on the process of acquiring colonial possessions later than the major powers. Like the Japanese, the Italians noted that most of the promising colonial territories were controlled by the British, French, Dutch, Portuguese and Spanish. The Italians managed to conquer Libya and Eritrea. In 1896 the Italians invaded the last black controlled state in Africa, Ethiopia. In a defeat that shocked the world, the Italians and their army were driven out of Ethiopia. The German statesman, Otto Von Bismark, stated that "Italy had a great appetite but weak teeth." This described Italian military prowess at the time.

Germany had a strong military tradition but was made up of many small kingdoms during the 19th century. Under Prussian leadership, Germans fought several wars to unify the German people. The most notable war being the Franco Prussian War of 1871. This resulted in the surprising defeat of the French, the unification of German people except Austria, the acquisition of Alsace Lorraine, and the hatred of the French.

Germans like the Italians and Japanese had been industrializing and German science and the educational system were the best in the world. Germany within 30 years of unification had bypassed the manufacturing capacity of Great Britain and was second only to the United States. Germany further embarked on an empire building effort resulting in gaining over a million square miles of territory in Africa, part of New Guinea, various islands in the Pacific and concessions in China.

German states for hundreds of years had been allies of Great Britain, and the British people were part German. The British Royal Family was mainly German taking the name House of Hanover. The Kaiser of Germany was in awe of the British Empire which ruled almost one quarter the entire globe. At the funeral of the United Kingdom of Great Britian and Ireland's King Edward VII in 1910, the German Kaiser wore an English Admiral's uniform to show his respect.

The Kaiser, much like many leaders including Theodore Roosevelt, was impressed by the American Alfred Thayer Mahan's recent book *The Infuence of Sea Power on History*. The book argued that a nation to be a great power must possess a powerful navy. The Kaiser wanted a navy as great as England and the United States. Since the English Navy was key to the safety of the island, a powerful German Navy was viewed as a threat to the British.

It was a great tragedy that despite the long history of friendship and similarity of peoples, the rise of German power and the building of formidable German navy close to England's shores made Germany the enemy of Britain. Even after the Kaiser limited the German Navy's dreadnought fleet to 60% of British forces, the English felt threatened.

As the 20th Century dawned, Europe or her children in America ruled the world. In Africa only Ethiopia was independent. In Asia only Siam, parts of Afghanistan and China were independent of the colonial powers. Latin America was independent but under the watchful eye of the United States and its Monroe Doctrine. The leaders in Latin America were white Europeans. Japan was an independent industrialized state, but it also was a colonial power. Russia had spread across Siberia subjugating numerous minorities.

Since the great regions of the world subject to a colonial conquest had been acquired by 1900, friction began to develop between the "have and have not" colonial powers. The powers with the less desirable regions began to eye the better regions controlled by the early colonial powers. The Japanese, Italians and Germans were pushing for more territory, yet the reality of the situation was that to gain more land the wars would not be against backward tribes or nations with far lower technology. Future gains if any would have to be made against mature industrial powers.

An example of this was the Spanish American war. The United States wanted to acquire Spanish colonies and succeeded in a short war. After "liberating" the Philippines from Spain, the United States fought against the Philippines that wanted liberty from America.

The Japanese fought a successful war against Russia in 1905. Russia was a first-tier colonial power with a second-tier manufacturing base fighting a war thousands of land miles from this base. The Japanese won and it shocked the world. Japan was an Asian country, in the eyes of Europeans, barely fit to govern itself. To the surprise of Europe, Japan had defeated Russia.

Theodore Roosevelt presided over the peace agreement. In the meetings U.S. representatives privately told the Japanese that their "Manifest Destiny" was on the Asian mainland and not the Pacific Ocean regions. This argument was simply an effort to get the growing powerful Japanese to vector their interest away from the United States colony of the Philippines.

The United State could argue decades later that it was the first colony to become a free nation and thus gain some cache with the new colonies. More disturbing for the United States and Europe was that Japan could argue that it was free of colonial rule and not European. That would later manifest itself in the Japanese "East Asia Co Prosperity Sphere" argument made by Japan. Japan's message to the colonies was that you can learn from Japan, we are like you, be like us under Japanese leadership. In the 1940's Japan would compete with America as the leader for Asian colonies and later the Soviet Union and China would join in.

The situation among the world's powers in 1914 was like a high school in which the more mature boys learned about girls or colonies ahead of the other boys. In 1914 the younger boys had grown up and had become stronger. Some became more powerful than the older boys. These "late bloomer" nations Germany, Italy and Japan wanted some of the action and a fight broke out.

Chapter 3: The Great War and the New Map of the World

The founder of Zionism in the 1880's was Theodor Herzl. His view seemed to be that the Jews could not find freedom as a persecuted minority in any nation except as the rulers of their own state. He argued that the Jewish people should seek diplomatic support among the European powers to acquire land in Palestine. The Ottoman Empire ruled Palestine. The Ottomans, sometimes referred to as "the sick man of Europe," were far behind the European powers in technology and population.

The Industrialized Europeans were so far ahead of the rest of the world that King Leopold of Belgium was given the entire Congo basin by European powers without the Congolese having any say. King Leopold proceeded to treat the Congo, an area a third the land area of the United States, and its people as his property to exploit. The result was an estimated genocide of 8-10 million Congolese people due to Leopold's drive to make a profit in the Congo no matter the suffering.

Theodor Herzl reasoned that eventually the Ottoman Empire would be broken up, and portions would be colonized by Europeans. His hope was to secure a Jewish homeland out of that banquet.

All it took was a spark and World War I was on. By 1916, the Allies and the Central Powers were at a stalemate. Germany allied with the Ottoman Empire and Austro-Hungarian Empires offered peace terms. My understanding is that each nation would return to their original border. The English were considering the terms.

Several factors may have affected the English decision to continue the war. First, the English had negotiated with the Italians, who were supposed to be allied with Germany and the Austrians but had stayed neutral in the war. The Austrians occupied territories coveted by the Italians, so the two nations were not natural allies. The British capitalized on this situation by offering this Austrian territory in the event of victory if the Italians would join the Allies in their war with Germany and her allies. Forty years later there is a quote reputedly by Hitler, not famous for his sense of humor. It stated that "Italy is the only nation to start each world war on the losing side but ended up on the winning side". The

British offered the Italians the Austrian territory along the Adriatic Sea, the Tyrol, and possible African colonies in return for Italy joining the Allies. It worked and the Italians entered the war on the Allied side in 1915.

A second factor was Britain's own interest in Palestine. The Zionist movement, led in Britain by Chaim Weizmann, lobbied for a Jewish homeland there, and British leaders had their own strategic reasons to want a foothold near the Suez Canal, astride the route to India. In 1917 the British issued the Balfour Declaration, announcing support for a Jewish homeland in Palestine at the expense of the Ottoman Empire. The motives were mixed: genuine sympathy in some quarters, imperial self-interest, and a wartime hope that the gesture might rally Jewish opinion in a collapsing Russia and a newly committed America to the Allied side. That last hope largely came to nothing, and historians still debate the weight of each motive.

Third, Romania, also bribed by territorial promises, joined the Allies in 1916.

In 1917 Romania was defeated by the Central Powers and Russia forced to make peace. The Germans now had their "place in the sun" if they could just finish off and win the war in the West. Russia gave up the Ukraine, Poland, portions of the Baltic States under the Treaty of Brest Litovsk to German control. German patrols were encountering Ottoman Empire military in the oil rich Caucasus region.

Against the sage advice of George Washington, the United State entered a European war and joined the war on the Allies side. The largest European group in America was German and yet the United States declared war on Germany and her allies. The reasons given were Freedom of the Seas and the Zimmerman Dispatch. Other reasons may have been the fact that the British controlled the transatlantic cable and thus could control the news of European events provided the United States. Because the British surface fleet ruled the Atlantic only British and French buyers could purchase American war material. Over time these purchases became a huge debt and American business leaders feared that if the Allies lost the debt would be defaulted on. Thus, support for an Allied victory.

In 1917 my grandfather, Jean Nelson, a first-generation son of Norwegian immigrants, was told by the media it was his patriotic duty to join the American war effort. Jean joined the United States Army Air Corps and learned to fly biplanes without a parachute at present day Lindberg Field in San Diego. The war ended prior to his deployment to Europe.

In the competition between the colonial powers, the First World War played out in this fashion. The existing or status quo industrial colonial systems survived. The French and British Empire gained territory at the expense of the Germans. Two of the new "late bloomer" industrial powers Japan and Italy gained marginal colonies at the expense of the other "late bloomers" Germany and Austria. The status quo powers gained territory at the expense of the Ottoman Empire and Germany. The Zionists via the British gained a toe hold in Palestine. Russia became the Soviet Union, a communist state, and lost Poland, the Baltic states, Bessarabia and Finland from their previous empire.

The dominant British and French colonial empires were increased but the war had cut the heart out of their military and their debts to the United States were immense. The "late bloomer" Italian and Japanese had gained some scraps of empire at the expense of the Germans and Austrians. The Italians and Japanese thought they deserved far more spoils from the war.

The United States became disgusted by the war. President Wilson had refused a British offer to take over Syria which went to French control. Canada had offered to buy the Alaskan panhandle and was turned down. The United States gained nothing except huge debts owed by the Allies that would never be paid. The human price America paid was over 100,000 deaths due to war and disease. The result of the war was the weakening of European powers, the birth of communism, and eventual fascism. The world had not been made "Safe for Democracy" as Wilson had proclaimed to encourage Americans into the war.

The Germans, burdened by the war debt and the terms of the Versailles Treaty which blamed them for the war, wanted a reversal and perhaps some revenge. When required to send their fleet to Scapa Flow to give to the British, the German Kaiser Liche Marine sailed their vessels to Scotland and then in defiance scuttled their ships. Some British then fired and killed Germans escaping on lifeboats. Germans cheered this act of defiance by their fleet. Years later the German Commander and his wife were killed by an intruder into their home. Their killer was never found.

Marshal Foch, the French Allied Commander, said of the peace of 1919 that it was a truce, and war would resume in 20 years. The Europeans ruled the world but could not divide it among themselves without fighting each other for the spoils. Would one more European civil war, weakening those nations, tip the scales of power away from Europe to the colonial nations? Should the European powers have considered their long-term adversary, their colonies with their burgeoning populations and gradual industrialization, or each other?

In 1928 Oswald Spengler wrote *The Decline of the West.* This German book noted the glacial changing of population and power between the mother countries and their colonies.

The colonies noticed. Gandhi in India observed. Mao in China noticed and so did Ho Chi Minh of Vietnam. Some of the colonial people had been trained and recruited into the mother country's army during the war. They were learning. As modernization spread to the colonies or developing nations, the technological gap began to tighten between colony and mother country.

More importantly, the mortality rates in the colonies were dropping due to improved food production and medicine. One example of the eventual result can be seen in Egypt compared to Germany in 1900 to 2025. In 1900, the German population was 70 million people and Egypt's was 8 million. In 2025, the German population was around 80 million and Egypt's was 90 million. In 2026, European people as a percent of world population declined to 9 per cent.

When the future Colonel Richard Evans was two years old the British leadership were forced to decide on a course concerning the key to their survival. They could not afford a naval arms race but were in a competition with the U.S. Navy in the Atlantic and the Japanese in the Pacific. Both Japan and the U.S. were allies of the British, but the U.S.

and Japan were becoming potential competitors and possible adversaries with each other in the Pacific Ocean and Asia.

Under American pressure the British did not renew their alliance with the Japanese Empire. Knowing that they did not have the productive capacity to compete with America in a naval arms race, the British further made an agreement to limit naval vessels on an equal basis with the United States. The British hoped for an American alliance. The Italians, French and Japanese were allotted smaller numbers of capital ships in the agreement. The Japanese lost face and were not happy. They thought the racist Anglo nations were ganging up on Japan which they were. Japan became more of a rogue nation in the late 1920s and 30s and followed the 1905 American advice concerning "Manifest Destiny". Japan pushed into Manchuria and China. They were temporarily halted by an eventual conflict with the Soviet Union in 1939 at the Battle of Khalkin Gol. Japan was seeking her "place in the sun."

The late bloomer Italians had over 400,000 killed in World War I. They were greatly disappointed by the spoils they received at Versailles. Italy received Trieste, some Dalmatian coastline, and the Austrian Tyrol. An editor and war veteran named Mussolini led a revolution of paramilitary super nationalists and took power. They called themselves fascist after the Roman symbol of fasci. Their movement was the architype for revolutions in Portugal, Spain, Hungary, Poland, Romania, Argentina and Germany. Even France adopted the form of government briefly.

Germany was in complete chaos in the early 1920s. The communists almost took control of the nation. Ultra nationalist Adolf Hitler attempted to take power in 1923 but failed. He was put on trial, gained some fame, and was imprisoned for a few years. In prison, he wrote *Mein Kampf*. In this book he demanded a new Germany with foreign policy aims of regaining the Russian territories won in 1917 but lost in 1919. He advocated a return to the German traditional alliance with Great Britain reasoning that the peoples were the same race with one nation a land power and the other a sea power. He predicted an alliance with Italy since Italy's foreign policy focused on gaining territory in mainly Africa and the Mediterranean Sea and thus did not conflict with German interests.

Hitler wanted to drive out Jewish influence within Germany and blamed Jewish profiteers for Germany's defeat in the First World War. He thought the Jews controlled German media and banking and that this power had to be broken. Jewish Karl Marx had developed many communist ideas. When Hitler took power, Jews in the West declared a boycott of German goods. This gave Hitler the excuse to hasten the destruction of Jewish retail businesses in Germany. Hitler hated communism or bolshevism as he called it. He wanted all Jews driven out of Germany. Hitler was in favor of a Jewish homeland. Hitler eventually made an agreement with the Zionists called the "Transfer Agreement" to facilitate Jewish immigration to Palestine. World War II ended this program but 50 percent of German Jews escaped Germany prior to the war.

In 1941, after the invasion of Russia, Hitler's persecution of Jews accelerated into the genocide we now call the Holocaust.

The Soviet Union toyed with the idea of a Jewish homeland along the Amur River on the Siberian-Chinese border, and the French at one point considered establishing a Jewish state in their colony of Madagascar.

Communist thinkers split over the question of nationalism. The internationalists, Trotsky chief among them, held that the workers' movement should rise above nations entirely. In the competition for power in Russia between the nationalistic Stalin and the internationalist Trotsky, the loser was Trotsky. The age of fascism demanded patriotism and nationalism. Stalin wanted to harness Russian nationalism to build Russia first and then spread communism. Trotsky wanted all people to give up nationalism and believed the force that would unite the movement was communism itself and the common goals and lives of the workers, the proletariat.

Chapter 4: The Road to the Second World War

My first American ancestors was the reverend John Lyford. He was an educated man and a minister. He was sent to the British Plymouth Colony in 1624 on the *Charity.* The minister did not have to fight Indians or work hard in the sun farming. He was sent to save souls. He was given a previously built home.

Rev. Lyford decided that the food and privileges were not being equitably divided within the colony. He is probably at fault for my mother's leftist leanings. Lyford asked the captain of a ship returning to England to carry a letter in which the reverend's complaints were stated. The suspicious captain read the letter and reported his findings to the powers in the colony.

My ancestor was then taken before a court and confronted with his treacherous act. He proceeded to beg for mercy and even burst into tears. He was forgiven and returned to his place of privilege. Months later he sent out another letter, was caught and banished from the colony.

This was not a good start for my family in America.

During the American Revolution Benjamin Franklin, whose son was a tory, predicted that someday the British Empire's heart would not be in London but in Philadelphia. Franklin was English and loved England. Franklin's relationship with his son illustrates the divided feelings Americans and British have toward each other. In a way, Franklin was correct for the power center of the Anglo-Saxon world is Washington, D.C. and not London. With the flood of Irish, German and Italians to America the relationship with Britain became more distant.

The British tried to snuff out our nation in the War of 1812. Failing at this, they tried to help keep it divided during our Civil War. This only made sense since we periodically threatened British Canada. We invaded Canada during our revolution, during the War of 1812, there was a small invasion attempt after our Civil War, and a planned invasion in the 1920s and 1930s. It is a fact that our Congress approved funds and began building two air bases for the purpose of invading Canada in the 1930s.

It was assumed that at some point the British and Americans would go to war over Canada and in the Atlantic Ocean.

The British in 1867 could see that the United States would be a Superpower, so they appeased the United States settling American Civil War claims in America's favor and making Canada a Dominion. This made it politically more difficult for the United States to invade Canada to "liberate it" from the British. American GDP passed the British Empire in 1871. When the U. S. made claims for Hawaii. which the British explored first and thus had a strong claim, the British backed down. The British relented to the United States over a dispute which almost led to war during the Cleveland administration over Venezuelan debt.

As America got stronger, Britain appeased America. As Germany became more powerful than the British, the English appeased the Germans up to a point. German population and production were greater than Britain by 1905. Was it a mistake for the British to not appease Hitler in his negotiations for the return of German Danzig from Poland in 1939?

What if France and Britain had avoided war with Germany over Poland by pressuring the Poles to relinquish the German city of Danzig? Wouldn't Germany and the Soviet Union have gone to war while the British and French watched? After those two titans battled it out, couldn't the West have then demanded a compromise and balanced peace agreement or threatened a two-front war? Instead, the half American half British Winston Churchill along with Neville Chamberlain and Lord Halifax managed to get Britain and France to fight Germany first. Was that an intelligent decision considering British history in Europe, the balance of power and the interests of their nations?

Shouldn't a declining power appease the rising powers and avoid direct confrontation? Great Britain was the third or fourth leading industrial and military power in the world in 1939 and yet attempted to run its diplomacy as if it still was a first level power. Is the United State behaving in the same manner today? Is it overestimating its power?

With war breaking out in Poland in 1939, my father Richard Evans became convinced that his country would eventually go to war. He had read Erich Maria Remerque's German book *All Quiet on the Western Front* about the slaughter in the trenches of World War I. My father wanted more than a rifle to fight and increase his chance of survival. He loved to fly.

Every young man in America in the 1920s and 1930s knew the story of Billy Mitchell and Charles Lindbergh. Mitchell had proved that air power could sink a battleship. Test were made on a captured German dreadnought, and sure enough Mitchell was able to sink it. He did cheat a little violating the test rules, coming in at lower altitude to make sure he hit the stationary target. It was later learned that the chances of a B-17 dropping bombs from an altitude of 20,000 feet on a ship moving 30 knots were next to zero. The solution was a dive bomber that could get to 1500 feet to hit the target. Much needed to be learned but Mitchell proved that a revolution in air power and warfare was coming. Mitchell speculated that a foreign power could someday strike the Hawaiian Islands. Everyone knew the foreign power was Japan. Mitchell criticized the army publicly and was court-martialed. We are likely witnessing a revolution in our time with smart weapons and drones that with artificial intelligence can precisely hit targets and coordinate attacks on the run.

I recall as a SAC Brat hearing my father and his friends speak with great respect and almost reverence for Billy Mitchell. In some ways, Mitchell was the father of the United States Air Force.

Colonel Charles Lindberg was somewhat of a martyr. He was the son of a congressman that voted against the United State entering World War I. In the early 1920s Lindberg was flying for the postal service. In those days there was no radar and radio was just developing. The accident rate was very high, so the pilots had to be excellent. Lindberg, as everyone knows, was the first solo flier to cross the Atlantic in 1927. He instantly became the most famous man of his time.

After the kidnapping and death of his son, the distraught Lindberg and his wife moved to Europe. While there he was honored at the United States Embassy in Berlin with the Service Cross of the American Eagle medal. The leader of the German Luftwaffe Herman Göring took great interest in Lindberg. He allowed Lindberg to visit German aircraft factories. Upon returning to America, Lindberg reported his findings to the U.S. State Department. He was greatly alarmed by the apparent lead the Germans had over the U.S. aircraft industry.

In May 1940, France's northern armies had been defeated by Germany and 240,000 British soldiers had retreated and escaped via Dunkirk. Approximately 100,000 French soldiers were also evacuated, but they returned to France to aid in the defense of their country. Very few British soldiers were returned to France to fight the Germans. The French were eventually defeated and almost 1.5 million French soldiers were captured and interned in German prisoner of war camps in Germany

Most of the world thought that England and Germany would make peace. Hitler wanted peace to allow him to focus on what he considered the red menace of Soviet Russia. His dream of the 1917 German Empire in Russia was yet unfulfilled. While after defeat in World War I, the Germans were only allowed a 100,000-man army, no air force and the surrender of their navy. The victorious Germans in 1940 had other plans for France.

In the Armistice Germany agreed to allow the French around a 100,000-man army in southern France and a 150,000-man army in North Africa. The French were also allowed an air force and full control of their navy. The Germans occupied Paris and the area of France along the English Channel and Bay of Biscay. The French fleet was the fourth largest in the world and was based in Toulon in Southern France with half the battleships in Algeria. The French Empire was still considerably larger than the United States.

The Germans told the French that once peace was made with England, all French prisoners would be released and the German Army would leave France except for German speaking Alsace Lorraine and Luxemburg, a small German speaking nation near Belgium.

Though Hitler signaled that he wanted British neutrality and a free hand on the Continent rather than the conquest of Britain, Churchill refused. Some in his cabinet, Lord Halifax among them, wanted at least to explore terms. The coverage of this period in movies and media usually implies Hitler intended to occupy England and make it "Nazi", but the record of the peace soundings provides no evidence of that. Few

Americans are aware that a negotiated peace was ever seriously on the table.

Ten days after the French and Germans made peace, France was a neutral in the war hoping England would stop fighting so that France could get its soldiers in German prison camps back and the hated Germans out of France.

Churchill against his admirals' strong recommendations order the British Navy to neutralize the French fleet in Algeria. Churchill claimed he feared the French would allow their traditional enemy the Germans access to the fleet and it would be used to invade England. The result was an attack that sank three battleships and killed an amount of Frenchman equal to 60 percent of U. S. losses at the Pearl Harbor attack. The French almost declared war on England but instead launched two air raids of 80 aircraft each to bomb British Gibraltar.

A week later, prior to the Battle of Britain, Hitler publicly made a peace offer to Britain. The same offer was made with a possibility of a Polish state. The catch here would be that half of Poland was occupied by the Soviet Union, and they did not want a free Poland.

Churchill did not respond to Hitler's offer. He had his deputy Lord Halifax respond. Halifax implied that the offer was a humiliation of Britain and that it was a demand. How was it to England's disadvantage to have negotiated and bought time? England needed time to rearm. What advantage did England give up if Germany would leave Western Europe and release millions of former soldiers back to their potential enemies. Hitler wanted a deal and was making all the concessions. No need for a Normandy Invasion and troops to threaten Germany if they became too successful in their planned war with the Soviet Union.

How did it hurt England or America to get back millions of soldiers and have the nazis and communists killing each other? Harry Truman said the same thing when he stated that if the Russians were winning in a Nazi fight, he'd help the Nazis and vice versa. Patton said the same when in 1945 he stated, "we fought the wrong people."

We do not know what political pressure was applied to Churchill, but we know that the City of London produced a lobby known as the Focus. One of its members owned Churchill's mortgage on Chartwell.

What if peace had been made in 1940? It is likely the Holocaust would have been less severe since Germany would seek good will with the West and allow a continuation of the Transfer Agreement.

In Halifax's radio response to Hitler's peace offer, Halifax stated that he would not even bother answering many of Hitler's points because they were so false as to not be worth discussing. How often have you seen the media pull this tactic to avoid a subject they want to avoid? What Hitler stated was three truths.

First, the British had planned in early 1940 to invade Norway forcing the Germans to get a one-day jump on them. The British goal was to shut off Swedish iron ore shipments out of Narvik, Norway in the winter by occupying that city. Second, the British had made an agreement with supposedly neutral Belgium to join the Belgians in fighting the Germans. Lastly, the British and French had based 200 bombers in Syria to fly over Turkey to bomb Baku, which produced 85 percent of Russian oil. Russia was supplying oil to Germany.

All these statements by Hitler were true. In fact, when the Norwegian King Haakon VII was awakened and told his nation was being invaded, he asked, "by whom?" The Turks told the British and French they would attack the bombers flying over Turkey. The collapse of France ended the plan to bomb Soviet Baku.

In war it would make sense to deprive one's enemy of iron ore or oil. That's what the British and French planned to do at the expense of two neutral nations. But Halifax was lying to the world and his people and a chance at an honorable peace was thrown away. The British and French whose empires ruled much of the world had the audacity to claim Germany wanted to conquer the world. Germany wanted its "place in the sun" at the expense of the Soviet Union.

The Battle of Britain commenced, and Lindberg and other Americans feared that Roosevelt and Churchill were maneuvering to get the United States in another European War. In August 1940 the American First Committee was established. The committee thought the British could make an honorable peace and that if the war continued there would be one of two results. Britain would lose and the British Empire would collapse. The British would win and the British empire would collapse with the Soviet Union overrunning central Europe or worse.

The American First Committee thought that if the European War would continue, the Japanese would be emboldened to attack European colonies in Asia or even United States territories to achieve their aims.

The committee thought that if the United States entered the war hundreds of thousands of American would die, debts would increase, communism would spread and the U.S. would gain little. They considered Hitler a lesser danger of evil versus Stalin. Roosevelt likely assumed the British Empire, which was approaching bankruptcy, would fall and the U.S. would regain via alliances and business the empire's territories. That is what happened. An empire that took over 300 years to build was destroyed within ten years of the end of the war. The British people had to live on war rations until 9 years after the war until 1954.

Some members of the committee were former President Herbert Hoover, future President Gerald Ford, Henry Ford and famous architect Frank Lloyd Wright. Future President John Kennedy did not join but contributed $100, which would be $2,500 today.

Richard Evans was a licensed pilot when he joined the Army Air Corps. His first military aircraft was the Boeing Stearman Biplane. By August 1940, he was learning to fly more advanced aircraft and sometimes training other pilots. Mike McCoy, future leader of the B-47 test program, decided to move to Canada to join the Canadian Royal Air Force. His goal was to learn to fly and fight in the Battle of Britain. Young men unaware of the conflicting political views made the decision to fight for what they believed was justice.

Meanwhile, their air hero Charles Lindberg was fighting to keep their nation out of war.

When Pearl Harbor was attacked, Lindberg petitioned Roosevelt to allow him to fight. Roosevelt, deeply angered by Lindbergh's isolationist stand, refused to allow him to serve in the United States military. The media spread rumors that Lindberg was a Nazi sympathizer. No one spoke of Lindbergh's spying on Nazi aircraft plants and that his German medal was awarded in the United States Embassy when the two nations were at peace. Charles Lindbergh eventually became an aircraft industry consultant to the military and flew numerous combat missions in the South Pacific. After the war, this controversial American hero became a consultant to the Chief of Staff of the United States Air Force and Pan American Airways. He spent most of his later years in relative seclusion in Hana, Hawaii.

PART TWO: SAC PILOT EXTRAORDINAIRE

Chapter 5: The Best Officer I Ever Knew

In this chapter I will provide an overview of my father's development into an Air Force Command Pilot and Officer. I should add that I encouraged him to write a book about his interesting life from his Tennessee years of childhood development to his interesting experiences during the Second World War. This book entitled *Richard Eager a Pilot's Story* was written by my father and partially edited and published by my sister. It is very true to my father's authorship though a few pages were changed. I understand why that was done but to maintain historic accuracy, I will point out the difference between my father's work and my sister's edition in this chapter. I heartily recommend my father's book for its many insights and terrific story telling of an important time in our nation's history. If you read the book, you will see why I am so proud to be one of his SAC Brats.

When Richard Evans was a child, the world experienced the Great Depression. Many Americans view the 1930s collapse as an aberration and the result of government policy errors. They are not aware that economic depressions have occurred as far back as the Dutch Tulip Mania of 1634. Records of economic history go back to at least the 1600s in England and France. The South Sea Bubble and Louisiana Bubbles of 1720 were disastrous for these cross-channel rivals. These two manias resulted in depression after their collapse.

The world experienced another depression during the American Revolution and the early years of the French Revolution. Evidence of this claim would be the fact that the largest corporation in the world, the British East India Company was bankrupt. The famous tax on tea was a subsidy by the British government to help the damaged company. The French Revolution was triggered by a default on that nation's national debt in 1789. The Luddite Rebellion, with its destruction of factory equipment in England, was likely a symptom of deflationary and depressionary conditions of that time. During the Napoleonic Wars the

English were forced to send 30,000 troops to the English Midlands to retore order.

Depressionary conditions typically cycle every three generations. The result was depressionary conditions in 1720, the 1780s, repeated in the 1840s, again in the 1880-90s and the 1930-40s. This cyclical viewpoint of history is the foundation of the Kondratieff Wave Theory. One aspect of the theory is the tendency for major political instability and war occurring after an economic depression. The goals and economic situation of the Germans, Italians and Japanese made those nations the disruptors of the status quo and the aggressive force bringing war to the world after the 1930's depression.

It was my father's fate to be a youngster during one of these turbulent times. Richard Evans' parents were college-educated people and his father was the principal of the high school in Knoxville, Tennessee. Richard Evans had three brothers, a dog, played football, went to church every Sunday and was an Eagle Scout. For a child growing up in depression, he experienced a modest but rather idyllic young life.

I once asked my father why he decided to join the Army Air Corps. He was a very brave man, yet he modestly told me that he had been impressed by two things. First, the excitement surrounding the Charles Lindbergh Trans-Atlantic flight. Every boy wanted to be like "Lucky Lindy." Richard Evans wanted a life with adventure and excitement serving his country.

Second, my father saw the German movie *All Quiet on the Western Front.* This movie depicted the personal level of killing that politics forced on young men. It showed industrial warfare such as artillery and machine gun fire impersonally destroying the lives of thousands of advancing men as if they were cogs in a machine. The movie was from a German viewpoint, but it did not matter as it became clear to anyone watching that these men did not hate their "enemies" and might have been friends if meeting under different circumstance. Human nature, perhaps cycles, and politics were dictating that the men would sacrifice their lives.

Young Richard Evans, facing a World War I type of war, decided to take the initiative and have some control and freedom over his fate. As a pilot within the cockpit of his airplane, he had some independence and control. My father reasoned that he would benefit with a machine that would help even his odds of survival. No need to charge with thousands into artillery and machine gun fire. Interestingly, after World War II ended statistics indicated that the survival rate for U. S. bomber pilot in Europe in 1943 was lower than for the U. S. Marines storming various islands in the Pacific.

Richard Evans, as a young man, suspected that his country was being drawn into the European War in 1939. He took a proactive stance. He learned about a class that offered free flying lessons to young men that scored the highest on a government test. He did not have money to pay for the course but sat in on the lectures. Eventually the professor noticed Richard and because several students had dropped out, allowed Richard to attend free of charge. Richard Evans was the last student in the group chosen. He was going to get free flying lessons.

After he soloed, the free lessons ran out. How could he continue to fly? Lacking money to rent an airplane or buy gas, Richard would offer to fly his friends around Tennessee for a fee. Perhaps this was the first airline in east Tennessee. My father would fly a biplane and land on golf courses to drop off his buddies. Once on a takeoff he had a failure and crashed. Fortunately, the aircraft was undamaged, and he was able to fly back to his home field.

After the fall of Poland to the Nazis and Soviet Union, Richard Evans was sworn into the U. S. Army. He was a good pilot but had to overcome air sickness to fly. In the summer of 1940, the world was shocked as the German Wehrmacht defeated the Dutch, Belgian, British and French Armies. The French Army was considered the best in the world at the time.

After the 240,000 British and 100,000 French retreat from Dunkirk, most of the French troops returned to France to continue the fight. The British decided they were in no position to do the same. The French government requested more British fighter aircraft to help in the continued Battle of France. The Churchill government refused fearing a further weakening of English fighter defenses would jeopardize the island.

The Germans could field 3 million men to the remaining French 2 million. Within weeks, the May/June war was over. Over 1.5 million Frenchmen were in German prison camps. Hundreds of thousands of Dutch and Belgian prisoners of war were also captured by the German army. To protect Paris from destruction, the French declared it an open city and sued for peace.

The Italians seeking to be in on some of the spoils from a German victory, declared war on France and made some minor inroads into the Alpine Provinces along the French Italian border.

When Germany lost World War I, she lost 20 percent of her land area in Europe, her Russian conquests, 1 million square miles of colonial territory in Africa, New Guinea and her central Pacific Ocean islands. Germany was only allowed 100,000 men in her army, could not have an air force and was forced to transfer her entire fleet to the British Navy.

While the Versailles Treaty was being dictated and an armistice was in place, Germany continued to be blockaded by the British Navy resulting in 500,000 mainly women, children and old people dying of starvation. Under threat of continued blockade, the German representatives reluctantly signed the agreement which demanded severe war reparations and the admission that Germany caused the war.

When the tables were turned with the fall of France in 1940, the French were forced to negotiate an armistice with the victorious Germans. They were somewhat surprised by the terms. Assuming the British would soon make peace, the French agreed that the Germans could keep the prisoners the Germans held until the war ended. The Germans allowed a 100,000-man French Army in France and a French Air Force. The French Empire was allowed to keep 150,000 men under arms in North Africa. The Germans did not demand French colonies, nor did they demand the surrender of the French navy, the fourth largest in the world. That navy was based in Toulon France 300 miles from the Armistice temporary border between German held France and French controlled areas. Five of the navy's battleships were based in Algeria on the other side of the Mediterranean Sea. The Germans occupied the French English Channel coast and the Bay of Biscay coast in an agreement ending once peace was restored with England. What remained of metropolitan France set up a new capital at Vichy and continued to control southern France and the vast French empire in Africa and Asia which was larger in size than the United States.

Hitler put out peace feelers with the Churchill government to end the war. During the Dunkirk Evacuation there was favorable discussion within Churchill's cabinet to make peace. With the successful evacuation of the bulk of the British Expeditionary Force, the British interest to continue the war hardened.

In June of 1940, the British government was virtually bankrupt and its only chance to continue the war was via continuing loans from the United States. The British Empire controlled 25 percent of the globe but had reached what Paul Kennedy would describe in his book *The Rise and Fall of the Great Powers* as "Imperial Overreach". The British Empire could not generate enough income to finance its defense. In our time have the United States' world commitments outstripped its ability to defend them? In the 1940s the United State produced 50 percent of world manufacturing. In 2026 the United States produces 12 percent.

The British Empire was like an aging blue whale surrounded by Orcas. The United States wanted the British Empire to end. The Americans wanted to control the North Atlantic, Canada and the Middle East. As mentioned previously, the United States built several air bases near the Canadian border in the early 30s for the purpose of invading that nation. America's army had a complete war plan to invade its northern neighbor in the 1920s and 30s. There was a real risk of war between the United State and Britain over the Atlantic Ocean in the 20s and 30s as power shifted from the British Empire to the United States.

The United States wanted to have non-tariff access for its businesses into the British Empire. The late bloomer Japanese Empire wanted British possessions in Asia. India, supported by American media, wanted independence from British rule. Italy wanted British Mediterranean islands such as Malta and Cyprus. Italy wanted British East African possessions and even the Suez Canal if they could be taken. The Soviet Union had an interest in driving through Iran to the Persian Gulf threatening British possessions in the Middle East. Even fascist Spain wanted to acquire British Gibraltar.

The nation England remained at war with; Germany did not desire the destruction of the British Empire. Germany wanted its sphere of influence to be eastern Europe including the Ukraine and the Caspian oil regions. If Hitler could reacquire a former German colony in Africa in negotiations with the British, the indications were that he would have been happy with that result. A return of all colonies lost in World War I to Germany was not the German focus. Eastern Europe was.

The Nazis would in 1940 and 1941 make peace offers to Britain and an alliance proposal in which German troops would be offered to defend the British Empire around the world. This was an echo of centuries of German British cooperation in Europe and America with Hessian troops. Hitler thought the British would be pleased that the Germans were keeping communism out of Europe via eventually opposing the Soviet Union. Hitler considered Great Britain a Germanic nation and a natural ally.

These thoughts were not well publicized in the United States. My father was taught that the communist Soviet Union which had also attacked Poland was a "work in progress" and not a threat to world peace. In the 1930s, as Germany took back prior German regions of Europe like the Saar, Rhineland, Austria, Sudetenland, Memel and Danzig Corridor, the media described it as conquests or an attempt to conquer the world. With hindsight we know that argument was not exactly the case. Even Czechoslovakia, which was absorbed by Germany, Hungary and Poland after the 1938 Munich Accord, had a history of being under German control.

To stay in power and in his view help his nation, Churchill began a process of friendly blackmail on Roosevelt. He ignored growing German offers for peace and territorial withdrawal and focused on what he claimed would happen if Germany invaded England. He speculated to Roosevelt that the British Fleet might then be controlled by the Germans. Churchill would then speculate on the situation in the Atlantic Ocean with the British, French, Italian and relatively small German Navies threatening America. Add to this the specter of an enemy Japanese Navy in the Pacific. This argument would then be followed by another request for loans and aid to fight the Germans and Italians.

In terms of world manufacturing the United States was by far the leader, followed by Germany, with Russia and Great Britain production equal. Japan and Italy were around 10 percent of U.S. production. France was around 15 percent of U.S. manufacturing.

When the French made an armistice with the Germans ending fighting in France in June 1940, Roosevelt expressed to Churchill concern that the French fleet would go to German control. This was an illogical stretch since the Armistice Treaty between the French and Germans stated that the French Navy would remain under French control. This fear was further unfounded since the border separating German controlled France and the main French naval port at Toulon was 300 miles. In the event of a surprise German invasion of the remainder of France, now called Vichy France, the French would have time to scuttle their navy. Approximately a third of the French capital ships were based 1000 miles from the border in Algeria. Speculation that the French who hated the German nation above all others would turn their fleet over to that nation was unfounded.

In 1942, to counter the Allied Landings in North Africa, the Germans occupied Vichy France and attempted to secure the French fleet in Toulon. True to their word the French scuttled their fleet to keep it out of German hands.

The British almost started a war between France and England. Churchill, against the advice of his admirals, ordered a British naval force to approach the French fleet based in Algeria and to demand the surrender of the portion of the French Navy based there. The French were now considered a neutral country in the ongoing war between Germans, Italy and Great Britain. There followed several hours of negotiations as each fleet communicated with their governments. The French position was that they were a neutral nation in the present war and had no intention as a sovereign country following the orders of admirals of another nation.

Churchill ordered the British Navy to open fire on their defenseless former ally's navy anchored at port. The result was the sinking of three battleships and the killing and wounding of French sailors at a level of around 70 percent of the American losses at Pearl Harbor a year later.

When my father Richard Evans read about this attack on a former ally by the British, the American media described the French as almost deserving the treatment. Since the 1940s United States media has regularly described French behavior in the 1940 Battle of France as subpar and the British as glorious heroes. Some of this is due to the brave British behavior in the Battle of Britain but this argument ignores French losses of almost ten times more men then the British, the British refusal to reenter the Battle of France and the British attack on their former ally's fleet. Prior to their evacuation at Dunkirk, the British lost a total of 5,000 soldiers to the French eventual 100,000. An additional 4,000 English soldiers were killed due to the sinking of an English troop ship during the escape from France.

From a French point of view, they had played a secondary role to the British and the United States in their diplomatic efforts to curb growing German power in the 1930s. This was sometimes done against the French better judgment for ultimately in a European war, France was stuck on the continent facing Germany while the United States and Britain were protected by the Atlantic Ocean and English Channel. The British pressured the French into forming an alliance with Poland against Germany. This reduced the chances of Britain, France and Poland of negotiating the return to Germany of Danzig. The German response was to invade Poland initiating World War II. The French joined the British in invading Norway in 1940 only to be forced to evacuate Narvik.

When the Germans invaded Northern France, the French supplied 2.5 million men to the British 300,000 troops. Since the British army left France via Dunkirk and did not send air force or army replacements to France, France was then defeated almost fighting alone. In French eyes the English, their former ally relatively safe in England, betrayed the French when attacking the French fleet. The French were furious and sent two air raids of 60-80 bombers to attack British Gibraltar. The French came close to declaring war on Britain.

The "devil is in the details" and my father's generation did not learn from our media of the French viewpoint until decades after the war's end.

Did the "Focus" lobby Churchill? Winston Churchill was a great writer and public speaker, but also an alcoholic and a chronic gambler who reportedly spent thousands of pounds a year feeding both habits. A brilliant and financially reckless man, he was rescued in 1938 by Sir Henry Strakosch, who was born to a Jewish Austrian family, and who took over Churchill's crushing investment debts and in time forgave them entirely.

Richard Evans was in the Army Air Corps because he loved to fly and he was being told by his nation's media in various ways that Germany was determined to conquer the world. As a patriotic American of partial Alsace-Lorriane German descent, he was training to do his best to stop them.

Adolf Hitler was no fool. In early 1940 the French Army was considered the finest army in the world. The Germans had defeated it in six weeks and had driven the British off the continent. The British and French were even attacking each other. Hitler wanted a secure western border which would allow his nation to attack the Soviet Union in a one front war. He knew that if the war dragged on the British naval blockade would starve Germany of the raw materials she needed as an industrial state. The Soviet Union supplied the raw materials Hitler needed but he correctly suspected that eventually the Russians would shut off the supplies and go to war with Germany. An early German victory over the Soviet Union would solve Germany's raw materials problem and remove the Soviets from the chessboard. Germany would then be self-sufficient which was Hitler's ultimate goal.

Hitler wanted peace with Great Britain and possibly an eventual alliance. He could then take what Germany needed from European Russia and begin his building dreams for Berlin, soon to be renamed "Germania." Hitler was likely aware of his deteriorating health which made him a man in a hurry. France and England could rule over the black and Asian peoples. Hitler wanted a land-based white European Empire from the Rhine to the Caspian Sea.

By the summer of 1940, the war in the West had reached a strange pause, and the question of peace was very much alive — more alive, in fact, than the histories I grew up with let on. On July 19, fresh from the fall of France, Hitler stood before the Reichstag and made what the

Germans called an appeal to reason, printed and dropped by air over England as "A Last Appeal to Reason." Its terms were vague by design, but the thrust was unmistakable: Germany claimed no wish to destroy the British Empire and wanted Britain out of the war, in exchange for a free hand on the continent and, above all, in the East.

That this was a real opening, and not mere propaganda, is shown by what was happening quietly in the neutral capitals and inside the British government itself. On June 17, the very day France capitulated, R. A. Butler of the British Foreign Office spoke with the Swedish minister in London, Björn Prytz, and after consulting Lord Halifax, told him that Britain's course would be governed by "common sense, not bravado," and that no chance of a reasonable compromise would be thrown away. Prytz reported this to Stockholm. The message was clear enough-the King of Sweden and other neutrals stood ready to carry soundings between the powers, and a part of His Majesty's Government, including the Foreign Secretary himself, was willing to listen. A negotiated peace in 1940 was not a fantasy of cranks. It was a live possibility, entertained at the highest levels of the British state.

It was Churchill who refused it. When he learned of Butler's conversation — British intelligence was reading the Swedish cables — he rebuked Halifax for language that smelled of defeatism, and he had already, in the tense War Cabinet meetings of late May, fought down Halifax's argument that Britain should at least discover what terms might be had. Churchill would not explore them. The popular story that Hitler's offer concealed a planned occupation of Britain has no support in the record. What Hitler wanted was British neutrality, not British conquest, but neutrality on his terms meant conceding him the mastery of Eastern Europe. Churchill would not put his name to that, least of all trusting a man whose signatures on the Munich Agreement had already proven worthless.

So, the peace was real, and the British turned it aside. Here my father's judgment, and mine, parts company with the history I was taught as a boy. Colonel Richard Evans came to believe, as General George Patton is said to have put it at the war's end, that "we fought the wrong people" and that the wiser course for the West would have been to take the paper peace and stand aside while the two great tyrannies of the age destroyed each other. Hitler's fixed purpose was an empire on Russian soil, while Stalin's regime was the one force that stood in his way. Let them grind each other down in the East, the argument runs, and the West could deal afterward with whatever staggered out of the rubble from strength, and at a fraction of the price. It is essentially the case Patrick Buchanan would later argue in *Churchill, Hitler, and the Unnecessary War.*

I will not pretend it was a safe bet, and neither did my father. It might have gone the other way. A Germany freed of a western front, unblockaded and resupplied, might not have bled to death in Russia at all. It might have won, seized the Caucasus oil and the Ukrainian wheat, and emerged not spent but enlarged, a self-sufficient empire from the Rhine to the Caspian that no later coalition could pry loose. That was precisely the danger Churchill saw, and it is a fair one. However, weigh it against what actually came to pass-Britain bankrupted her Empire and lost it within a generation, and the Soviet Union finished the war holding half of Europe behind an Iron Curtain. It took forty years and the whole apparatus of the Strategic Air Command to hold the communist back. My father judged the gamble worth taking. Reasonable men disagree, and many do. But a SAC officer who spent his life deterring the very Soviet power that the war had left astride Eurasia had, I think, earned the right to ask whether the West had chosen its enemy well.

The Battle of Britain began in July 1940. It is well known that the British were able to use radar to avoid being surprised by the Luftwaffe sorties. The Royal Air Force had the further advantage of fighting over their territory. A RAF pilot shot down over England, could be quickly patched up and placed in a new aircraft. A German pilot shot down over England either died or went into an English prison.

The ME 109 was likely a slightly superior aircraft when compared with a Spitfire or the older Hurricane fighters employed by the British. The Germans had the edge during the Battle of France. What the English had in the Battle of Britain that the Germans lacked was high octane fuel. The Germans learned that the English fighters were traveling 15-25 miles an hour faster than months earlier. The reason was excellent fuel. The concept was developed by two chemists, Polish Herman Pines, and Russian Vladimir Ipatieff. Both had immigrated to the United States prior to the war. Their ideas were incorporated into the United States oil industry, and Ethyl was born. The Germans never had high octane fuel during the war. When asked what the most valuable Lend-Lease item transported to the Soviet Union by the United States, Stalin said, "aircraft fuel."

Hitler consistently hoped that he would not have to send his army across the English Channel to invade Britain. The German naval leaders would not consider an invasion unless their Air Force had complete superiority over southern England. Hitler was more focused with the coming struggle Germany would have with the Soviet Union. One result of this view was that Germany with the resources of Western Europe produced fewer airplane than England in 1940.

Idealistic, volunteer pilots from all over the world moved to England to fight the Germans. One man from America was Mike McCoy. Mike would someday be my father's superior in the Air Force's B-47 test program. Mike would lead the development of the B-47, the first jet aircraft designed to fly to another continent via midair refueling, bomb a target, and return home. Since America was not in the war, Mike moved to Canada and joined the Canadian Royal Air Force. After training, Mike was moved to England to fight in the Battle of Britain.

After the British attack on the French Navy in Algeria, Hitler was seriously considering a German attack to capture British Gibraltar and then closing the Western Mediterranean from British Naval traffic. He sent Admiral Welhelm Canaris, chief of German intelligence to meet with the Spanish leader Francisco Franco. Franco owed his position as Spain's leader to the efforts of Germany and Italy in helping Franco's forces in the 1939 Spanish Civil War. While Canaris was a World War I-decorated German patriot, he was a monarchist and secretly very anti-Nazi. He informed Franco that Germany would lose the war and that Franco should not allow German troops transit through Spain to attack Gibraltar. Hitler was completely unaware of this betrayal and met a month later with Franco with the idea of having Franco's Spain join the Axis and helped take Gibraltar. Franco proceeded to make all sorts of demands needed before going to war. Eventually Hitler was so frustrated that he broke off the meeting. A week later, while meeting with his Italian ally, Mussolini, Hitler stated that he would rather spend an afternoon with a dentist than with Franco.

Franco would manage to stay out of the war. He would send approximately 50,000 troops in the Blue Division to fight in the Soviet Union near Leningrad, German U-Boats might visit Spain, and Spain helped smuggle in rare minerals for the German war industry. While all the European fascist leaders were eventually overthrown, only Franco and Salazar of Portugal would survive into the 1960s. After the war, Spain became an American ally. Eventually there would be three Strategic Air Command Air Bases in Spain. They were Moraon, Zaragoza and Torrejon.

Ultimately, Hitler's planning focused on his long-term goal of building a German Empire on Russian soil. Hitler looked at the Battle of Britain, Gibraltar and North Africa as side shows to his objective of a Ukrainian/Caspian Sea basin Empire. This statement is backed up by the fact that Germany had a maximum of 150,000 troops in Africa verses 3,500,000 soldiers fighting in the Soviet Union during the war.

As the Battle of Britain was raging in August 1940, Captain Evans was flying the B-17 Flying Fortress bomber. His flight training began at Love Field at Dallas, Texas and was furthered at Randolph Field in San Antonio. The B-17 was given the name "Fortress" because it was arrayed with eight 50 caliber machine guns on the aircraft.

The aircraft was initially marketed to the Department of War as an anti-shipping weapon. In 1938 future Air Force and SAC leader Curtis LeMay was able to navigate a B-17, 500 miles off the coast of the United States and intercept the Italian Ocean Liner Rex. This mission was made to prove the ability of the bomber to intercept foreign navies far out at sea to protect the American coastline. Ironically, while the B-17 was used extensively in the eventual war with Japan in the Pacific, the aircraft likely only sunk one Japanese destroyer during the entire war. It was initially given some credit for the U.S. victory at the Battle of Midway, but evidence showed the victory was due to the bravery and skill of United States Navy dive bomber pilots.

The B-17 with its range, bomb load and firepower became the workhorse of allied bombing in Africa, Italy and Western Europe. Prior to the U. S. entry into the war, it was thought that the B-17 and B-24 bombers could fly into Axis defended Europe, fight their way past Nazi fighters to the target, accurately drop their bomb load and return to base. The reality of that hope was to be far more difficult.

During the Battle of Britain, the English and Germans had initially avoided bombing civilian targets. The Germans focused on daylight bombing of airdromes, aircraft factories, radar sites and other Fighter Command targets. The idea to either destroy in the air or on the ground the British Royal Air Force. The only hope that the Germans had of invading England was total air superiority. Otherwise, the combination of British naval power and some air power would isolate any German invasion force. The British had the further advantage of a partial breakthrough of the German military code.

The British, lacking a heavily defended bomber and fighter protection attacked German cities at night, mainly killing civilians. The Germans had avoided bombing London but on one occasion accidentally bombed within the city's limits. Churchill likely knew this was a mistake but took advantage of the situation. He ordered an immediate night bombing of Berlin. At first, Hitler ignored what he viewed as a provocation and did not respond. Churchill ordered seven further nightly bombings of Berlin to provoke Hitler. At one point, a frustrated Churchill was quoted by future French Premier Charles de Gaulle as pointing to the sky and saying, "why won't they come, why won't they come?"

Why did Churchill apparently want his capital city and its civilians bombed? The likely arguments were first that it would divert the German attempt to destroy Fighter Command and thus remove any idea of a German invasion. Second, with the German offer of peace many Britains and Americans thought Churchill was foolish not to end the war. With the greater damage and intensity of the war, more people would become angry and less likely to want to make peace. Third, the very suffering and stories of bravery of London people would bring sympathy from key nations to join England, particularly the United State. The media took care of this as chain smoking Edward R. Murrow reported the Blitz to the world. There was no equally sympathetic media coverage of the suffering in German cities due to nightly bombing.

When Hitler took the bait and bombed London, he lost his remote chance of winning the Battle of Britain. Except for perhaps the atomic bombing of Japan, assisted by the Soviet Union's defeat of Japanese forces in China, bombing of nations has never forced and ending of a war. In 1940, the Germans were learning that bombing alone would not end the war. The British and Americans would learn this lesson in 1943-45 over Europe and years later over Vietnam.

In my father's book *Richard Eager a Pilot's Story,* his modest early life is described. He grew up with three brothers, a religious mom, and school principal father in Knoxville, Tennessee. He had a wonderful childhood and was mentored by some very fine people. For a lad in the Great Depression, he was very fortunate.

Since I was only a "gleam in my father's eye" I cannot bear witness, but from what I learned, life as a young captain in the United States Army Air Corps was pretty good. Add to that, Richard was a pilot. When you look at pictures of him with his Air Corps hat cocked a bit to the left, he looked like a Jimmy Stewart/Clark Gable character. Richard Evans was not a tall man like his 6-foot older brother Pug. My father was 5 foot 9 inches and built like a lean gymnast. I think my father had some sensitivity about his height, and this made him more successful and a "hard charger." You must love that overcompensation drives us.

If you read his book, his modesty, fairness, and honesty come through. He told me many times about how we all want credit and appreciation. He taught the lesson that the most powerful way to market oneself and garnering that acclaim we all need was by letting the "other guy be the winner." This can be seen when a quarterback on a football team is interviewed and all he speaks about is how well his front line and team did in the game. The audience or people in general can see how the quarterback played, but he gains further kudos by praising the "other guy." In contrast the quarterback that praises his own performance even a little, loses ground with his audience.

Richard Evans was a fine man and was naturally generous with others, but he also knew that the most selfish thing one could do to promote oneself was to praise the "other guy."

You may recall the movie *Top Gun* and the scene in which the strong young pilots are playing volleyball on the beach. If you can call men "beautiful" these boys fit the bill. A similar narrative happened at a swimming pool near Woodlawn Lake in San Antonio, Texas, in 1941.

Chapter 6: A Courtship on the Edge of War

There was a young girl, age 15, named Jo Ann Nelson reclining by the pool with her girlfriend, Lois. Jo Ann was a Texas girl, half English and half Norwegian. She was a beauty and later became a primary model for Catalina Swimwear. Jo Ann appeared in several Hollywood movies and did several photo shoots only with the year's Miss America and Miss Universe on Catalina Island. Jo Ann's granddaughters were all lovely. One would become Miss Texas in 2015 and go to Miss America and then a few years later win Miss Florida 2020 in the Miss Universe contests.

Captain Richard "Eager" Evans and a wingman walked onto this scene. Shirts off, stomachs tightened, standing straight to look taller and eagle eyeing for any attractive women around the pool. My father was age 20. Richard was a pretty good diver. His specialty was a one-and-a-half with a full twist. After seeing Jo Ann, he proceeded to announce his presence with his specialty dive. It did not work. She did not look in his direction. Like a bird doing a dance to get the attention of the female, my father did another dive. Again, no luck.

Richard Evans was a resourceful man. He remembered how Glenn Cunningham rose to the occasion and overcame his fear and rejection to become the world's best runner. My father's answer was to strike up a conversation with Jo Ann's best friend sitting by her at the pool. I cannot tell you how the conversation went but somehow Richard ended up visiting Lois the next week, and Lois lived next door to Jo Ann.

"All is fair in love and war," and America was close to going to war, so Richard did not have a lot of time. After visiting Lois briefly, Richard ratcheted up his courage and went next door to Jo Ann's home. Jo Ann's mother, my grandmother Florence, answered the door. It was lucky for my father and me that my grandfather, Jean Nelson, was on a business trip. Jean would not have gone along with his young daughter going out with a 20-year-old pilot. Jean had been a biplane pilot in World War I and Jean knew about pilots.

My father was a very polite young man and having been raised in the church in Knoxville this tendency was noted by Florence. Captain

Richard Evans won over Florence and thus his girl became Jo Ann Nelson.

I recall well the feelings of being a young man, experiencing freedom from my parents' home, being concerned with how I would earn a living and being in love. I do not recall thinking that I would soon be in a war since Vietnam was winding down when I graduated. My father's generation faced a World War. This was the fear of my father's generation. The young men had to face that danger. I do not mean to understate the Korean or Vietnam Wars, but the scale of those wars was small when compared with what America faced after Pearl Harbor. The young women faced the maiming or death of a husband with possibly children to raise alone.

As a young pilot, able to afford a car with a pretty girlfriend to see on the weekend, my father had made it. He even impressed his girl by doing a B-17 fly by her high school one time. I learned later that my uncle Tom did something a lot more fun.

In the spring of 1941, Hitler had made the decision to invade the Soviet Union and secure his long-term war aims. That was to destroy communism in Europe, secure the resources of the Ukraine and Caspian basin. Most of the nations bordering the Soviet Union feared the Russians far more than the Germans. In the Spring of 1941, Hungary and Romania joined the Axis. The Bulgarians and Fins drew closer to Germany for protection.

Italy foolishly had attacked the British in Egypt and were defeated by the English in 1940. This forced Hitler to send German forces led by General Irwin Rommel in 1941 to rescue Italian Africa interests. The Italians further complicated the war by attacking Greece and then being driven out of Greece. The Germans were forced to invade Yugoslavia, Greece and Crete to stabilize the situation in the Balkans prior to their planned invasion of the Soviet Union.

It has been argued that the Italian failed invasions forced a delay and reduction in the German forces needed to defeat Russia in 1941. Some historians argue that the German invasion of the Balkans to bail out Mussolini delayed the German attack on the Soviet Union by two critical weeks. Others argue that the winter of 1941 delayed the drying of the roads in Western Russia and the Ukraine so that the German attack was also delayed. We will never know. We know that the Germans were banking on a fast campaign. When it bogged down near Moscow and became a war of attrition Germany was in trouble.

American industrial capacity has been allowed to decline drastically over the last 40 years. The result is that our military has a shortage of conventional weapons. After weeks of expending weaponry in any war the United States is at risk of running out of ammunition. This results in United States military doctrine emphasizing short wars. The Germans had the same problem in World War II. What will be the United States chances of success in a war of attrition or a war of production?

The United States spent 50 percent of its Federal Budget funding our military under John Kennedy. Now we spend 15 percent. Since we do not have a draft as in 1960 there are less funds in the limited budget available for new equipment.

In May of 1941 Britain continued to face the might of Germany and Italy. The Soviet Union was assisting Germany but planning for war with Germany expected in 1942 or 1943. The United State was not fighting but sending Lend-Lease aid to the British. German and British bombers were nightly bombing each other's cities. General Erwin Rommel had defeated the British Desert force in April capturing its commander, General Richard O'Connor.

The motivation of Rudolf Hess will always be unclear. Hess was the Deputy Fuhrer of Germany. He was nominally the successor behind Göring in the event Hitler died. In the most remarkable act of the Second World War, Hess flew at night a Me 110 fighter to Scotland with the goal of brokering peace between Germany and England. He sometimes had to fly 50 feet above the waves to avoid radar detection. He flew within 10 miles of his target, the home of the Duke of Hamilton who Hess had met at the 1936 Olympics. Hess turned his aircraft upside down and parachuted to the ground.

While Hess thought of himself as a diplomat trying to bring peace, he knew that he could just end up in an English prison. He left a letter for Hitler telling him that Hitler could disavow the flight if Hess failed. Hitler later did just that since the British rejection of the flight made

Germany appear too anxious for peace and therefore weak. Hess offered the same terms as the July 1940 offer plus the Germans giving up recent conquests. Churchill would not even meet with Hess and had him placed in an insane asylum.

Churchill knew from Ultra intercepts that the Germans were preparing to invade Russia. It is hard to understand why Churchill did not make peace in either 1940 or 1941. His decision kept him in power but doomed his nation to an accelerated decline from first power to third power status. Within ten years the empire that Drake, Nelson, Wellington, Clive and Kitchener had built over 300 years was gone.

Was Winston Churchill a great leader? Churchill, a man that wanted to drop anthrax and poison gas on Germany in 1944, is considered one of the greatest men of the 20th Century. Hitler had nerve gas and refused his generals' advice to use it in Normandy. Some historians give him credit for the refusal due to his personal experience with mustard gas in World War I. It is more likely that Hitler did not use this terrible weapon out of fear that the United States and Britain also had nerve gas. They did not.

Meanwhile, a man that could fly without ground navigational aid 500 miles sometime 50 feet above water at night and was the number three man in the German nation was insane? A man that wrote that he could not sleep at night often due to the thought of German and English children being bombed to death in their homes was insane? A man that wanted the English to make peace and allow Germany to destroy Russian communism was insane?

What did the Allies eventually do with Hess? He was "tried" at Nuremberg at wars end. Decades after the last Nazi tried had been executed or finished prison terms, Hess stayed in prison in Berlin. At age 93 he supposedly hung himself while being guarded by either American, French, British or Russian guards. Hess's son had an autopsy done on his father and concluded that his father was strangled.

When Hess flew to Scotland, Richard Evans was doing extensive training in all-weather instruments flying across the Southwest United State.

On June 22, 1941, Operation Barbarossa began. We all know how it ended and most people understand that almost 30 million Russians died. Since 400,000 Americans perished in World War II, the Russians in comparison lost 70 people for every single American death. At war's end the Soviet Union would be one of two superpowers on earth. It would control central Europe and have the largest army in the world. The communist Russians would have tremendous influence in China and Korea. By 1951 they would have the hydrogen bomb.

In the summer of 1941, the United States occupied portions of Iceland and Greenland to aid the British in the Battle of the Atlantic. American destroyers were assisting the British Navy in hunting down German U-Boats. Hitler thought it was just a matter of time before the United States would declare war on Germany.

In July 1941 Japan occupied French Indo China. Japan could see a rare opportunity to gain the resources and empire her ambition over the last 100 years sought. The Europeans were fighting among themselves and did not have the resources to challenge Japan in the Pacific Ocean. Japan would do to the Dutch, British and French Empires what the Dutch did to the Portuguese hundreds of years previously. Japan would do what the British did to the Dutch two hundred years before. Japan would replace those nations as the new colonial master. The "late bloomer" had come of age. Only the U. S. stood in Japan's way and America was almost at war with the other "late bloomers" Germany and Italy.

What if Japan had won their war? Imagine the power of a nation that controlled China, Korea, Taiwan, Indo China, the Phillipines, Indonesia and Japan. While it can be argued that German power could be balanced, a successful Japan would have been a true superpower. While Japanese industrial power in 1941 was far below the United States or Germany its potential with an expanded empire was a tremendous threat. Hitler was aware of this when he stated his mixed feelings after his ally Japan conquered Singapore from his enemy the British.

A 1941 American Gallup poll indicated that 60 percent of Americans did not want war with Germany. Charles Lindberg and the American Firsters continued to argue for peace between the British Empire and

Germany. President Roosevelt's nation was no "late bloomer" and could argue it had led the colonial moves for independence. America was a colonial power holding the conquests from Spain and the Hawain Islands.

The United States had passed laws to fund building of air bases to invade Canada, sold used 50 destroyers for valuable Caribbean bases and build air bases to secure the Western Hemisphere. Was it positioning itself to take over European rule in vital areas around the world? Was Roosevelt only attempting to restore a balance of world power fearing German/Japanese dominance of Eurasia would threaten America? Perhaps both.

Roosevelt, while communicating with the American people that he did not want war, made a decision that brought the United States into the war. In 1941, the Unites States produced 80% of the world's oil and Japan was a major buyer. After the Japanese occupation of Indo China, the Dutch, British and Americans announced the ending of oil sales to Japan. Japan could either kowtow or go to war with America.

It can be argued that once Japan attacked Pearl Harbor and the Germans failed to take Moscow in December 1941, the Allies had won the war. It was a matter of manufacturing weapons, transporting troops and many people losing their lives. There would be reverses in Russia at Sevastopol or Karkov. The British would lose Singapore to a force half their size as well at Tobruk. The U. S. would lose the Philippines and be defeated at Kasserine Passs in Africa. The outcome was not in doubt. These were the views of my father Richard Evans at the time.

In 1942 millions of American men were joining the military. Captain Richard Evans job was training those men that wanted to become pilots. He also continued his training in the developing technique of instrument flying.

My father's book, *Richard Eager a Pilot's Story,* does a wonderful job of describing his life until the end of World War II. I hope you read his excellent book. I will add a small amount of background to his World War II experiences.

Jo Ann and Richard Evans at the pool

Chapter 7: Into Combat

In 1942, the United States was beginning to send bomber and fighter crews to England. The 8th Air Force was being built up in the preparation for daytime "precision" attacks on Germany and her industrial and military targets. The two work horses for the operation were to be the B-17 and B-24 bombers. Both carried multiple .50-caliber machine guns for defense and were expected to fight their way to the target, drop their bombs on the target and return. Due to the limited range of Allied fighter aircraft and the distances involved, a large portion of these operations were without fighter protection.

The United States Army Air Corps put a lot of confidence in a new computer weapon called the Norden bombsight. Crews were told in the event of a crash landing to destroy the invaluable equipment. It was claimed that the Norden could drop a bomb in a "pickle barrel." The view was that once the United States Air Corps could place enough day bombers over Europe, it could destroy the Nazi ability to wage war. Early in the bombing campaign the Germans captured a few of these Norden machines and the Germans were not overly impressed. They did not bother to tell us though.

In the summer of 1942, the 8th Air Force executed its first bombing raid of Rouen, France. The lead pilot was Paul Tibbets of later Enola Gay fame. Tibbets would be one of the men visiting the B-47 program and skiing with my parents in Tampa ten years later. Major Frank Perigo would lead the first P-38 squadron to England. Frank would be a dear friend of my father and the best man in Richard Evans' marriage.

Captain Evans was a well-trained pilot instructor. He wanted to join the "Mighty Eighth" based in England. He learned about a group of B-17's preparing to fly to England and join the war. Richard Evans volunteered to participate and command a B-17. Instead of sending the wing to England and joining the 8th Air Force, the U. S. government decided to invade North Africa. Thus the 15th Air Force was born in Africa.

Chapter 8: The Desert War

The American invasion of North Africa was a complex operation with considerable political intrigue. The French government in 1940 initially thought the war was going to end quickly. Churchill had refused a negotiated peace agreement in 1940 and 1941, though a faction of his own government had favored exploring terms. Now the war had broadened to include the Soviet Union and the United States. The Vichy French in the summer of 1942 could see that the odds of victory had swung to the Allies. They wanted the Germans out of their nation, to preserve their empire and to hopefully be identified with the winning side.

The movie *Casablanca* is a great propaganda piece as the Frenchman Louie tries to navigate between the pressure of the local German advisors and the Free French. The American neutral Humphrey Bogart must decide whose side to take. There is a scene in which a French patriot is killed in front of a poster with the name of the President of Vichy France. Another scene had a Bulgarian women speaking of her escape, yet Bulgaria was allied with Germany and annexed part of Greece. The British, hated by the French for the destruction of the fleet at Algeria, are never mentioned in the movie. There is even a well-played singing battle in the bar. Louis, the man whose country was on the fence, symbolically choses sides and eventually kills the German leader. Bogart tells Louis "This is the beginning of long friendship" as *La Marseillaise* is played. The message is that France will join its old friend America to destroy the Nazis.

If the British had invaded French Morocco or Algeria in 1942, the Vichy French Air Force, Navy and 150,000-man army would have fought. The decision was to make it the American invasion of North Africa. With the American-French history of friendship, planners thought the French less likely to resist.

The Americans planned to land in various areas with some British soldiers discretely thrown in. Since the landing force in the first week would only be 130,000 troops versus 150,000 French, the United States military was keen on increasing its odds.

This was achieved in two ways. First, American General Mark Clark was smuggled into Algeria via submarine to meet with Vichy French generals to make an agreement for an unopposed American invasion. Clark should be praised for his bravery in taking this risk. Secondly, Vichy French Admiral Darlan was contacted and informed of the possibility of an invasion. Darlan was the admiral that had to witness the British destroy part of his fleet in 1940. He was the number two man in the Vichy government. The Allies offered to put him in charge of the French government in North Africa if he cooperated. Charles de Gaulle, leader of the exiled free French, did not know of this arrangement.

In November 1942, the United State Army, with some British soldiers dressed in American uniforms, invaded French North Africa. The local French troops, unaware of the prior agreement made with Admiral Darlan, managed to kill around 250 United States servicemen. Darlan flew to Algeria coincidentally prior to the invasion to visit his son who was seriously ill with polio. Darlan ordered the French to stand down. French troops in North Africa obeyed and quickly changed sides. The Germans, sensing treachery from their viewpoint, invaded southern France. When the Wehrmacht arrived to capture the French fleet in Toulon Harbor, it had been scuttled by the French. As promised to the British in 1940 the French did not allow the Germans to take their ships.

Admiral Darlan had delivered on his promise to minimize French resistance to the North African landings. Admiral Darlan had kept his word, but had he outlived his usefulness to the Allies? De Gaulle was enraged. The American public had only been told part of Darlan's history. Our media depicted him not as a French patriot but as a Nazi collaborator that had changed sides. How could America make such an unscrupulous deal and place a man like Darlan in command of the largest group of French forces on earth? Did the Admiral have to go? A week later he was assassinated. The Free French in North Africa had a speedy trial, and the killer was executed less than three days after the killing. This ended the problem.

My father, Richard Evans, flew to Casablanca and later stated in his book that he saw the movie *Casablanca* in Casablanca at the new Casablanca theatre.

What about General Mark Clark? Churchill thought he was fantastic and that the very impressive Clark looked the part as a General Officer. General Clark led the delayed breakout of the Anzio beachhead in Italy in 1944. Since the beachhead was north of the German lines, Clark it is argued by some, should have moved across country to cut of the thousands of German troops to his south. This supposed failure allowed over 100,000 German soldiers to escape north to form a new line and fight again.

Why did Clark make this decision? Only he knew but some historians think that Clark wanted to be remembered as the conqueror of Rome. Did he opt to head north to capture Rome and perhaps glory and miss the opportunity to isolate a large formation of German troops? He received far less media publicity than likely to be expected since he captured Rome two days prior to the D-Day Landings in France.

Chapter 9: Montgomery's Pilot

In my father's book, he describes why he was granted the honor of being Field Marshal Bernard "Monty" Montgomery's pilot. I think my father believed this story but with further information this may not be the case. You can decide. The narrative was that Montgomery made a bet with General Eisenhower that Monty, as he was nicknamed, could advance his 8th Army past the German defenses along the El Mareth Line in Tunisia by a certain date. When Montgomery's Army succeeded, he demanded that Eisenhower pay up.

Eisenhower, who along with General Patton had B-17s to fly them about, claimed he did not recall the bet. Montgomery insisted and got his B-17 reward with crew. Being Monty's pilot meant that the crew would continue their bombing missions but had to be available to fly to any location to chauffeur the Field Marshal were ever he needed to go. It could be to Cairo, Algiers, Gibraltar or even London. In this way Captain Richard Evans became Major Richard Evans and was able to fly 55 combat missions plus ferry the commander of the largest British Field Army about.

My father developed excellent respect and friendship with Montgomery. Richard Evans would sometimes rotate his crew, and this applied to the Monty shuttle service. Montgomery once noticed that my father had a different crew and asked about them. Major Evans confessed that those men had gone on a mission with a different pilot and had been lost. Montgomery was a very decent man and was very remorseful to hear what had happened.

What is another version on why Montgomery a British Field Marshal was driven about with an American crew in an American aircraft?

In 1941, prior to the United States declaring war on Germany and Italy, America had an embassy in Rome. Italian spies had a key to the embassy and late at night broke into it. They cracked the safe and copied the United States diplomatic codes readily available. When the German sent the Africa Corp and General Rommel to North Africa in 1941, the Italians began to provide information from the U.S. source. The Germans eventually broke the code on their own as well.

The United States was giving immense aid to the British in Egypt whose army faced Rommel's in Italian Libya. The catch was that Roosevelt wanted daily reports on the situation on the ground concerning the British German struggle in Africa. Army Major Bonner Fellers was the American Defense Attache in Cairo. He was assigned the duty of monitoring and reporting on British military operations in the Mediterranean and Middle East Theatre. The British granted Fellers complete access to their activities and information. He dutifully reported everything he learned to his superior in the United State, where his reports were read by President Franklin Roosevelt and the G-2 section of the War Department General Staff. The Italians were also able to read and share Major Fellers' reports within 8 hours. The most secret Black Code data on British strength, position, losses, reinforcements, supply, situational plans, morale and related intelligence was communicated.

Within hours of transmission, Rommel had the information. Hitler called it the "Source" while Rommel, with a better sense of humor and some English knowledge, called it my "little fellers." Each day Rommel would ask of his intelligence people, "do you have any little fellers for me?"

It is well known that the British broke the German code or Enigma. They were able to read instructions from Hitler to Rommel. For example, Rommel was instructed to stay on the defense when he arrived in North Africa in 1941. Rommel would receive daily "little fellers" about the front and decide on his own to take advantage of the situation. Hitler due to the distances and the knowledge of the "Source" allowed Rommel considerable leeway in when to disobey an order. Hollywood media in the United States does a silly job of describing German military leadership as lacking initiative. Germans are depicted acting like robots obeying Hitlers every command. While Hitler held a tight leash on his military after 1943, there are many instances even post 1943 in which German troops disobeyed orders due to their view of the situation on the ground. Usually, they were not punished.

German General officers suffered by far the greatest percent of casualties because they "led from the front". In contrast, Allied generals gathered at communication centers miles behind the lines. Common sense and initiative were the great strengths of Wehrmacht.

As in all organizations, common sense could be lacking in the German Army. During the initial phase of the German attack on the Soviet Union, General Heinz Guderian was often disobeying the orders of his superior General Von Kluge. Kluge, repeatedly disturbed by Guderian's high risk taking, told Guderian, "your operations always hang by a thread." Guderian was the pioneer of the combined arms or Blitzkrieg tactics that had brought the Germans so much initial success. General Von Kluge became so angry with Guderian that Kluge went to Adolf Hilter and asked if Hitler would be his second in a proposed duel between Guderian and Kluge. Hilter put a stop to the fighting between the two men. It would have been wonderful for the Allies if Guderian and Von Kluge killed each other in a duel in 1941.

The British, due to Ultra intercepts, where caught assuming Rommel would not attack while Rommel had data about where the British were weakest. General Rommel, on his initiative, would disobey the orders and attack. Both his superiors in Berlin and his British opponents were then surprised. Rommel may not have deserved the "Desert Fox" nickname. He was a fine general, but he had an ace up his sleeve.

After the capture of Tobruk by the Germans, the British Commander Ritchey was replaced by Field Marshal Gott. Gott flew from place to place in a British transport plane called a Bombay Troop Carrier. The aircraft had no machine gun defenses. Gott was landing at an airfield near Alexandria prior to the Battle of El Alamein and suddenly not one, but six ME109s showed up over the field. Gott was shot down and killed. The story sounds so much like the United States military shooting down of Yamamoto. We had information about where and when he would land. We sent out several P-38's and shot him down. I would wager that few Englishmen familiar with the desert war are aware that the Commander of the largest English field army, the 8th Army, was killed by the Germans.

Field Marshal Montgomery replaced Gott. Did the code breaking allow the Germans to know Gott's plans or was it a coincidence that six fighters showed up as he was about to land? Did Montgomery prefer flying in combat areas in a transport aircraft or the faster B-17 armed with eight .50-caliber machine guns? Perhaps the story about the "bet" was a cover story.

During the Second Battle of El Alamein, New Zealand troops overran a German intelligence position at the front. That position was listening for "little Fellars." The intelligence officers were killed and the code books captured. After that Rommel flew blind. It is interesting to note that when Rommel moved inland to attempt to flank the British 8th Army at the Second Battle of El Alamein the British were ready. They were still listening to the Ultra code and Rommel, lacking his "little Fellars" advantage, had no alternative than to follow orders and be defeated. Rommel was outnumbered in almost all military categories by the British two to one at El Alamein.

FYI Why were we Americans surprised by the Germans at the Battle of the Bulge? After all we were reading the German codes. The answer is that the Germans had been pushed into their prewar territory and were mainly communicating over their telephones. The Ultra traffic was low thus the surprise.

Bonner Fellers eventually went back to Washington and was given a medal. He later was Deputy under General McArthur in administering the Japanese recovery after the war.

There is another interesting story concerning the reason that General Patton was dismissed from command in Sicily. The media narrative was that Patton while visiting an army hospital became enraged with two men suffering from shell shock. Patton as the story goes slapped the men a few times and called them cowards. All this is apparently true but there is another less known story about Patton that may have provided a more powerful argument for his dismissal.

Prior to the invasion of Sicily, General Patton gave a speech designed to fire up his troops. Patton indicated that no prisoners should be taken if our troops were "200 yards" or closer to the enemy.

America soldiers murdered 71 Italian and 2 German prisoners on July 14, 1943. The men had been captured and forced to take off their shirts and shoes to prevent escape. They were machine gunned in two cases by a GI and an American Army officer.

When Patton's deputy Omar Bradley learned of the murders, he reported them to Patton. Patton's reaction was to attempt to hide the incident. He saw no gain in reporting a crime that could not be corrected. Patton thought that reporting the incident would hurt the Army's reputation and might cause German reprisals. General Bradley persisted and made a report. In the court martial trial of the two murderers, the GI received 14 months in prison. The officer was acquitted but later killed in combat. Both men's defense focused on Patton's previous orders concerning taking of prisoners though in both cases the men murdered had already surrendered. The Biscari Massacre, as it was called, never made the newspapers out of fear of German and Italian reprisals. Were Patton's ruthless speeches and attempts to cover up the incident the reasons for his removal? Did his slapping of two GI's cause the removal? Perhaps both?

British Field Marshall Bernard Montgomery and Major Richard Evans

The aircrew of the Theresa Leta

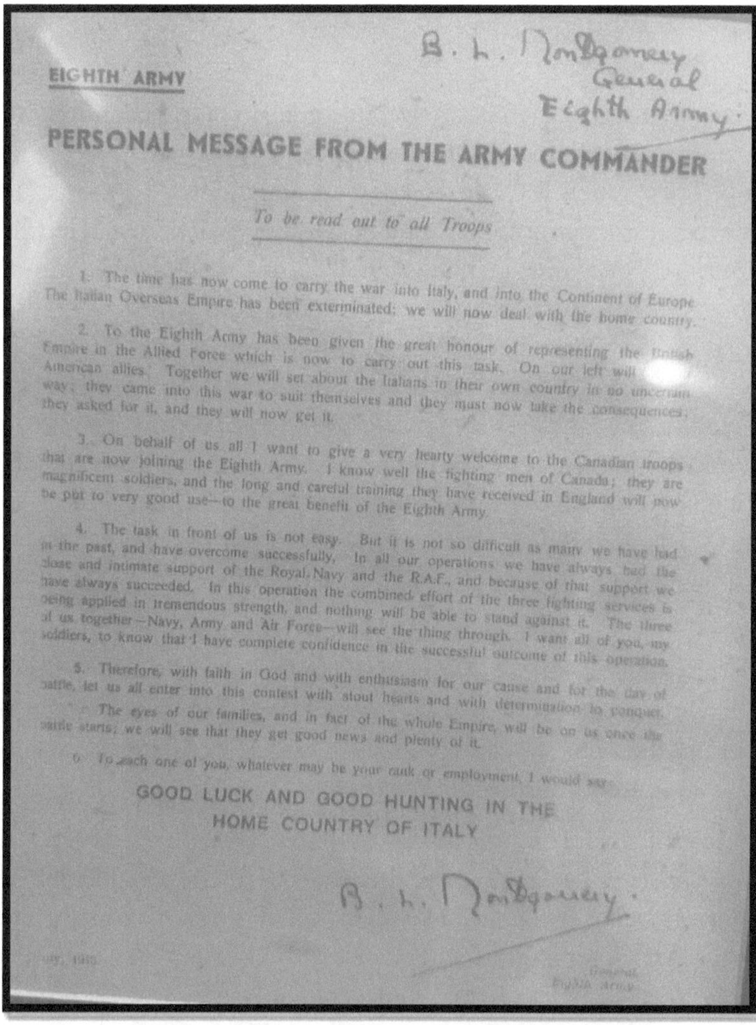

B. L. Montgomery
General
Eighth Army.

EIGHTH ARMY

PERSONAL MESSAGE FROM THE ARMY COMMANDER

To be read out to all Troops

1. The time has now come to carry the war into Italy, and into the Continent of Europe The Italian Overseas Empire has been exterminated; we will now deal with the home country.

2. To the Eighth Army has been given the great honour of representing the British Empire in the Allied Force which is now to carry out this task. On our left will [illegible] American allies. Together we will set about the Italians in their own country in no uncertain way; they came into this war to suit themselves and they must now take the consequences; they asked for it, and they will now get it.

3. On behalf of us all I want to give a very hearty welcome to the Canadian troops that are now joining the Eighth Army. I know well the fighting men of Canada; they are magnificent soldiers, and the long and careful training they have received in England will now be put to very good use—to the great benefit of the Eighth Army.

4. The task in front of us is not easy. But it is not so difficult as many we have had in the past, and have overcome successfully. In all our operations we have always had the close and intimate support of the Royal Navy and the R.A.F., and because of that support we have always succeeded. In this operation the combined effort of the three fighting services is being applied in tremendous strength, and nothing will be able to stand against it. The three of us together—Navy, Army and Air Force—will see the thing through. I want all of you, my soldiers, to know that I have complete confidence in the successful outcome of this operation.

5. Therefore, with faith in God and with enthusiasm for our cause and for the day of battle, let us all enter into this contest with stout hearts and with determination to conquer.

The eyes of our families, and in fact of the whole Empire, will be on us once the battle starts; we will see that they get good news and plenty of it.

6. To each one of you, whatever may be your rank or employment, I would say:

GOOD LUCK AND GOOD HUNTING IN THE HOME COUNTRY OF ITALY

B. L. Montgomery.

[illegible], 1943.

General,
Eighth Army.

Signed order for the allied invasion Europe (Sicily)

Chapter 10: What the Record Won't Say

I want to address the historic record in an area in which my father's book printed may be in error. I am referring to his emergency landing in Palermo, Italy. When Richard Evans first copyrighted his book (1989), he went to great lengths to describe his landing at Palermo. He told me this story, and he wrote in his original book that General Patton was present at Palermo Airport to meet General Montgomery and his staff on the B-17. In Carlo D'este's book on Patton Richard Evans ("the pilot") is given credit for saving the lives of all those on the aircraft. That can only make my family proud. In the book edited by my sister, she went to some lengths to indicate Patton was not present at the airfield. This was done in good faith because other sources indicate that Patton was at Palermo Castle at the time.

Richard Evans eventually died of Alzheimer's, so it is possible my father's memory failed him in this matter. That was my sister's view considering other versions. This is the only change she made to his work. She is likely correct, but it seemed to me that his version should be in place and in the unlikely case a historian wishes to pursue the matter he can view all sources to learn the truth.

There is a final error that likely should have been changed. In the book *Richard Eager a Pilot's Story*, there is a reference to Field Marshal Montgomery being the first Allied Commander to win a major victory against the Axis. This is simply an error. British General O'Conor in 1940 not only forced an Italian Army, four times his army's size, to retreat 500 miles but captured 130,000 prisoners. Soviet General Gorgy Zukov at the Battle of Moscow December 1941 likely won the entire war by smashing the Wehrmacht and forcing the Germans into a protracted war. Lastly, the Battle of Midway in July 1942 destroyed 40% of the Japanese Navy's entire carrier arm and killed many of its best airmen. Field Marshall Montgomery was the first British Commander to defeat a German army in World War II in November 1942.

After completing his tour, Major Evans was anxious to come home. Field Marshal Montgomery was kind and asked Evans if he wished to continue his duties, but my father wanted to return to the United States.

There was an incident between Gibraltar and London which was interesting and showed how skillful the German could be. A German agent supposedly spotted a man that looked like a double of Winston Churchill boarding an aircraft in Gibraltar bound for London. Also on the flight was the British actor and officer Leslie Howard who played Ashley Wilkes in *Gone with The Wind.* As the aircraft entered the Bay of Biscay, German fighters shot it down.

My father really admired the British 8th Army and its people. He found the men brave, generous and cheerful with the Yank and his crew temporarily attached to their force. The troops would sometimes go out into the desert to catch some extra protein to mix with their dried eggs.

There was a bird like a grouse that they would hunt without firearms in North Africa. My father said that he was invited to join some men for a hunt. They would drive around in a jeep until they spooked a bird. It would then run or fly low across the ground for several hundred yards. The Brits would follow the bird with a jeep and as they reapproached, off the bird would go but each time a shorter distance. After a few rounds of this, the poor creature was exhausted

The hunters would just strike it on the head with a cricket bat and toss the bird into the bag.

Chapter 11: The Brothers at War

Major Richard Evans returned to San Antonio to learn that his favorite brother, Tom, was being threatened with a court martial. Tom was an excellent pilot and like many of the men his age, had a wilder side. He and some of his buddies enjoyed practicing dive-bombing American farmers. They did not drop bombs, and the behavior was excellent training. They would spot some unfortunate farmer and pretend the horse and farming equipment was a tank. They would then dive on the farmer in their aircraft to practice. They would terrify the farmer and likely his animal if he had one. There were a few complaints filed by farmers in the area.

Tom's error was that he dove too low. His target saw Tom's aircraft tail number and wrote it down. Then the farmer filed a report. The training command knew his pilots would pull these stunts and had decided to make an example of someone. Training accidents were a problem in all the services and the leader of the training center wanted this behavior to stop.

Major Evans dropped in to visit the leader of the training program and made a pitch to save his brother. The officer started out by saying, "Evans, I know you are back from combat, and I would love to give you some slack, but your brother has got this coming." Major Evans asked how much longer Tom had until graduation. The answer was a week or two. My father's pitch was simply that his brother would probably get killed in combat and why waste the governments money spent on training him without sending him on?

My father never told me this story. Tom told me. Tom went on to have a proud record of service. He ended up fighting, dive bombing and strafing Japanese troops in the Burma Theatre. His plane was nicknamed the "Sunday Punch." Coincidentally, the aircraft had been purchased by people in his hometown of Knoxville by Sunday overtime work. A chapter of the World War II book entitled *We Were There* was written about Tom Evans and his aircraft. Tom and his aircraft are shown on the cover.

All four of the Evans brothers who served in the Army Air Corps survived. They were Colonel Bill Evans (B-29 pilot), Colonel Richard Evans (B-17 and B-29 pilot), Major Tom Evans (B-25J pilot) and Captain John Evans (B-24 navigator).

Lt Colonel Richard Evans and his brother, Lt Colonel Bill Evans

Captain Tom Evans and Sunday Punch aircraft

Major Richard Evans and brother, Captain John Evans, at Tinian

Chapter 12: The Long Way Home

At the end of World War II, Richard Evans was stranded in Okinawa with an assignment to ferry a B-29 to Delhi, India. He was to return to Okinawa via another aircraft and await a troop ship to go home. Evans noted orders which allowed a specific General a *carte blanche* to travel around the world within the Air Corps system. My father found it rather easy to change the recipient from General to Major Richard Evans. Everyone was trying ways to get home but my father did not want to embarrass his boss, so he told him about his plans. The response was pretty much that my father was on his own. Richard Evans had spent ages 20-26 as a pilot for his country and wanted to go home to see his wife and baby daughter.

Word of my father's travel plans spread around the base. A few buddies and his boss drove a truck out on the field to wave Evans a safe journey as his B-29 took off the runway. Even the control tower knew of his rebellion and wished him well.

When my father arrived in India, he attempted to use his new orders to keep traveling west. Next stop Karachi, then Cairo, on to Algiers, then to Casablanca, Dakar, Belém, Manaus, Caracas and Palm Beach. The local commander was no fool. He ordered Major Evans under house arrest in the officer's billeting. He would await the next aircraft back to Okinawa and get on a troop ship home.

Tennessee lads are resourceful, so after checking into officer's billeting, my father walked out to the flight line. Eighteen B-24s had just flown into the base and the crews were walking toward Evans. My father spoke with the commander of the squadron and asked for a ride. The commander asked if Evans was checked out in the B-24 which was affirmative. It seemed that one of the pilots had injured his foot and was unable to pilot the aircraft. Richard Evans volunteered and indicated that he had done considerable flying in the Middle East and North Africa.

Thirty years later, I was a lowly airman in uniform, stuck at the Andrews Air Force Base terminal and hoping to hitch a ride to Los Angeles. The terminal was packed with people with the same idea. In those days, it was not difficult to walk onto the airfield. Having previously worked in a control tower environment, I was comfortable there. I knew a flight was arriving to refuel before continuing to the Air National Guard airfield in Van Nuys, California. Remembering Major Richard Evans's exploits in New Delhi, I walked onto the field, saluted the pilot, told him I was from California, and asked for a ride. He pointed me to a master sergeant who was the loadmaster. The sergeant told me to board the plane. A few hours later, I was serving coffee to the passengers of the C-130 on my way home. One great aspect of my United States Air Force experience, whether as a SAC Brat or a lowly airman, was that if you were respectful, did the job, and kept a good attitude, people gave you some slack.

Major Evans bid farewell to Delhi, India. The squadron knew about my father's orders to return to Okinawa but in those days the important thing was to get the job done. His job was over, his associates knew how many years he had been in the Air Corp and they did not begrudge Richard Evans' efforts to get home. Over the Persian Gulf, which was the border of the India and Middle Eastern Commands, with the co-pilot at the controls of my father's aircraft, they had a mock ceremony. The bomb bay doors were opened, and Richard Evans tore up the Indian Command orders instructing him to fly to Okinawa. These orders were then dropped over the gulf with a bit of cheering and laughter. Days later my father returned to America and his growing family.

In 1946, Lieutenant Colonel Richard Evans age 26 was leaving the Army Air Corps. He retained his Reserve Status and embarked on a career in finance. Within a few years into his new career as an insurance agent, he was asked to speak at industry conferences about his new success.

PART THREE: A SAC BRAT'S STORY

Chapter 13: Birth of a SAC Brat

With little fanfare, this future Strategic Air Command Brat arrived in his home in Pasadena, California on October 29, 1948, the 19th anniversary date of the Wall Street Crash of 1929. Years later, when I realized the date, I just knew I had to be in finance.

This SAC Brat did not know he was going to be a family member of the Strategic Air Command let alone a Brat. I grew up in the post-World War II world as the men came home, when many used the GI bill to get college educations, built suburbs and enjoyed the American dream with growing families. The military services had integrated, and the various former European colonies were beginning to shake off their masters. The idea of building a new colonial empire was dead. Soon most of the former colonies had greater populations than the mother countries. Many of the colonial men had fought alongside soldiers of the Mother Country. These men had weapons and many knew how to use them.

There were two major powers on earth with the United States producing half of all manufactured goods in 1950. The Japanese, Italian and German nations were disarmed and focused on rebuilding their domestic industry under the trading umbrella and protection of the United States. Soviet Russia dominated central Europe and there was great risk that the rest of Europe would go communists. China, North Vietnam and North Korea were going communist.

When I was age three the Soviet Union and the United States both had nuclear weapons and were competing for world leadership. The United States offered capitalistic socialism and the Soviets dictatorial communism. The Soviet model tended to appeal to the developing nations that had been colonies. The dictatorial nature of a command economy made it more difficult to vote out or overthrow versus through a capitalistic socialist society common in Western Europe.

The Zionists were able to form the state of Israel at the expense of the Palestinians living in the region. There was great sympathy for their cause due to the suffering Jews went through during the war. In 1948 the

Secretary of Defense James Forrestal was asked if he supported the formation of Israel as a state. He stated that though he was not firmly opposed he saw no reason for the United States to get involved. He reasoned as an American nationalist strictly interested in the well-being of America that American support for Israel would hurt the United States. Forrestal thought the Arabs would be angry with the United States and that we needed their friendship with the coming struggle against communism. He wanted to protect American access to Arab oil and the Suez Canal.

The United States media roasted him. Great political pressure was brought to bear on President Truman to fire Forrestal. Six months later Forrestal was removed from office. The media reported that Forrestal was suffering from depression, had lost weight and was placed in a navy hospital for observation. He was expected to stay at the hospital for a few weeks and regained six pounds according to his brother. A few days prior to his release James Forrestal jumped out of the 14th floor of the hospital.

When I was three, the Korean War broke out. The United States struggled to contain aggression. Some analyst thought the war was a diversion to get America focused on Asia which would allow the Russians to overrun Western Europe. NATO was being formed but it faced a mobilized Warsaw Pact of perhaps 3 million troops with less than half that number. The United States was not trying to push out communism. It was trying to contain the system and someday push it back.

America could have huge expensive armies all over the world or find another way to deter communist aggression. The other way was to be willing to use nuclear weapons on an enemy that attacked our allies or our country. Thus, the Strategic Air Command or SAC was born.

My father did not have to return to the Army Air Corps which had become the United States Air Force. He had certainly done his part to support and defend the nation he loved. He was making excellent money, and his wife was modeling and she was participating in a few Hollywood movies. He was living the dream life in Southern California, even with a country club tossed in.

Why did he reenlist? First, because he was doing business with ex-military guys and some of them were going back into service. He felt guilty if he did not join in. Second, he was a patriot. Third, his buddy Colonel Don Hillman called him and asked if he would like "the best job in the Air Force." Now Lieutenant Colonel Evans was to move to Tampa, Florida and work under Colonel Mike McCoy to develop the new B-47 jet bomber. There would be a need to develop a midair refueling capability since the aircraft's range was only 3,000 miles. This aircrafts job would be to be able to fly to the Soviet Union and drop a nuclear weapon anywhere in that nation. This capability would hopefully dissuade the aggressive expansionists policies of the Russians and the Chinese.

What did Mike McCoy, the boss, and Colonel Evans, his deputy, have in common? Both had worked with the British and in the B-47 refueling program a partnership was being developed using the British and American crews. British air bases would be critical for success. I confess no one ever told me why they asked my father to leave civilian life to rejoin the Air Force, but I think I have the reason. Mike McCoy had fought in the Battle of Britain and Richard Evans had kept safe the British most famous military leader of the 20th Century. They both knew and respected the English, and the British would respect them.

I do not recall anything about my childhood and home in Pasadena, California. I do recall my mother dropping me off at the bus stop to go to the preschool at MacDill Air Force Base in Tampa, Florida. I went to preschool for three years. I was a "Butterfly" the first year, a "Blue Bird" the second year, and then a "Busy Bee." "Busy Bees" were supposed to be busy getting ready for first grade. I recall at graduation being the only kid to go all three years. My beautiful mom loved me, but she was not the most domestic person I ever knew. She continued to model for Catalina and later joined my father at the Cypress Gardens Ski Show on weekends.

In the early 1950s there was an expression about kids that they should be "seen and not heard." Our parents knew the air bases were safe for children, so the Brats ran all over the place. The culture was geared to the father's career, and boys had an advantage over the girls in that society. You could walk anywhere except the flight line, and no one would even notice you. This gave the SAC Brats a great deal of independence and confidence. I had no contact with civilians while at MacDill. They did not share the bond, did not attend our schools and what their parents did was silly and unimportant. Our fathers were protecting the whole country. We could walk out to the flight line fence and see our fathers screaming off a runway. In a theatre we would see a couple of young airmen in flight suits with a small suitcase near the exit. If given a signal they had to get out on the flight line, take off, risk their lives and go bomb Russia. What could the civilian kids admire versus our fathers?

The life was hard on families. There could be long separations and occasionally we would learn of a divorce in a family we knew. Worse was the fact that the accident rate for high-performance aircraft was high. I had three friends who lost their fathers in airplane accidents and one on a damn Florida golf course due to a lightnings strike. My father's boss Colonel Mike McCoy crashed a B-47 near present day Orlando International. You will note the field is named McCoy Field to this day (MCO). Mike was flying in a test program with an English pilot and moments later both men were dead.

The accident rate in the B-47 was over 10 percent. That represents 200 airplanes and many crews lost their lives in peace time. Later my father was the first Air Force pilot to fly the challenging Mach 2 B-58. The Starfighter F-104 had a 31 percent crash rate and was nicknamed "the widow maker" by flight crews. A huge problem with high-speed aircraft was to balance out the tons of liquid fuel sloshing around inside the aircraft. In a sharp banking turn the liquid could cause an unbalanced and uncontrolled aircraft.

My father described one takeoff with a B-47 that he almost crashed. The takeoffs were against the wind, and he was accelerating his aircraft north away from Tampa Bay. The result was that he had some difficulty clearing the trees at the end of the runway. It was a warm moist day with light rain and water on the runway. Colonel Evans' aircraft tanks were completely full of high-octane fuel. The takeoff attempt was not JATO a Jet-Assisted Take-Off, which helped overloaded aircraft into the air by providing addition thrust in the form of small rockets attached to the plane. Richard Evans told me that his aircraft reached takeoff speed but as he attempted to leave the runway the aircraft felt like the water on the runway was holding it down. Having passed the point of the runway on which the flight could not be aborted, Evans' aircraft lurched on toward the trees beyond. At the last moment the aircraft ripped free of the runway suction and barely cleared the trees.

Colonel Evans set the 35-hour record for keeping a jet aircraft aloft. This was accomplished day and night via refueling tankers miles above the earth. A problem with the prop driven KC-97 tanker was that it moved so slowly that if a B-47 came up to the fuel boom for a fill up the B-47 was going to slow and would stall. To refuel, the KC-97 had to angle itself on a crash course with the earth to build up enough speed to allow the B-47 to get a drink without staling. This problem was rectified by the jet powered KC-135. I later learned our friend Colonel Trimble arranged for a bed made of two by fours to be available near the navigator's area to allow the pilot and crew some rest during the record attempt.

If you were a pilot on a B-47 over the ocean and you could not refuel you were going to crash into the ocean.

The kids or Brats were great fun. One of my best friends was Stevie Hillman. His father became a general and in the early 50s flew B-47s sorties over Soviet Air Bases taking surveillance photos. For his heroism, General Curtis LeMay presented Don Hillman with his second Distinguished Flying Cross for the secret overflights of the Soviet Union. He told Don that no one should be told why he received this honor. Years later the story was allowed to be told.

During World War II, Don was an ace fighter pilot and pulled off one of the great escapes. He was shot down over Germany and sent to a prison camp in east Germany. Don made a deal with a German guard that if released, Don would try to help get the guard into the United States to live and be a citizen. Both Don and the guard were concerned because the Red Army was approaching their prison.

Don was released and acquired a scrawny cow which he led with a rope like a farmer walking across Germany to American lines. Don Hillman kept his promise and helped his German friend come to America. The German ended up settling in Seattle, Washington and his son went to the University of Washington. When Don became an elderly man, he retired back to Seattle and lived a few miles from his old friend, his German prison guard.

Don's son Stevie was mischievous but lots of fun. My Dad told me a story about Stevie in which Don and my father had just flown back from a training mission with the B-47. Don was proud of the very nice soft top convertible auto he owned. When Don returned home Stevie was using the top like trampoline. The result was a stretched-out top that slumped two feet down into the car. I recall spending the night at Stevie's and being terrified because his father had a dead polar bear rug with a big head and teeth. That night I was awakened by the feeling of slime on my face and hair. Stevie as a joke cracked an egg and was dripping the contents on my face as I slept. I heard that another time he got a glass of orange Kool Aid and told his sister it was gasoline and chased her with a lighter in his hands.

Years later Stevie had a serious accident when his father was commanding the B-52 wing at Roswell Air Force Base. He was fooling with a shotgun and almost blew his entire upper arm off. It was saved and repaired when I visited him. During my visit, Steve and I decided it would be fun to toss a smoke bomb near the front guard gates station. Our little smoke bomb ended up 30 feet behind the guards' post and was so weak that the guards did not even see it. I am glad they didn't. Stevie had the wickedest laugh and would cross his arms after he pulled something on you.

When we were four- and five-year-olds at MacDill, our parents would drive ten miles up Dale Mabry Highway to Lake Carroll. Don Hillman and my father both had ski boats at the officer's clubhouse on the lake. On weekends our parents and their kids would all go out on the lake. Don and my father built a ski jump on the lake and all the officers would enjoy going over the jump. Stevie and my job was to push water up the front of the jump which when mixed with the wax on the hot wooden surface made the jump slick. It is amazing how our minds recall things from the past. I can almost feel the hot surface of the jump as I write this. Our fathers would then come barreling in and fly over the jump.

Steve and I would then hide out in the front and higher end of the jump's underside and fish. We would catch bluegills using kite string, pressed bread and safety pin. Sometimes we would hear a boat coming and would stick our heads out above the end of the jump and then duck down when our parents hit the lower starting point of the jump. Then you would hear a *wamp* and see a backside view of your parents flying over us and landing in the water 50 feet from the jump. I cannot imagine what it looked like to our parents as they approached the bottom of the jump and saw their kids' faces knowing that if those kids did not duck down, they'd lose those faces. This was a time when parents trusted their children's interest in self-preservation. Kids had BB guns, but no one lost an eye.

While my father broke his arm on the jump, I was the only kid to get hurt fooling with the jump. The kids would play hide and seek with airplane inner tubes around the jump. My place to hide was using a tiny air pocket under the barrels beneath the jump. It was so tight that I hooked my toe inside one of the metal bands that encircled the barrel to the jump. This combined with the body's ability to be stable in the water allowed me to stay unseen without any movement. Then I kicked free to swim in. The result was that I almost sliced my second toe off. I recall swimming to shore and the pain when I kicked. As I stood on the white sand beach, I could see all my blood in the sand. I had to go to the hospital on that one and get a novacaine shot right in the wound. It was still better than what Steve went through.

Our house was 400 yards from Tinker Elementary School. I recall part of the distance was across a gravel area with large Florida stickers. Since I loved to run around barefoot, I was always stepping on a tack. The worst were the Florida stickers. They were very sharp. You would get them stuck to your foot and could not pull them off since they would stick to your fingers.

I was both successful and a failure at Tinker Elementary. My first-grade teacher, Mrs. Nelson, picked me out of the class to represent the school in the annual Gasparilla Parade. Gasparilla was a Spanish pirate that lurked out of Tampa Bay centuries before and for some reason he was honored. Each elementary school picked out a first grader and sixth grader to represent the school. I did not like getting picked because it required my mom to sew a silky pirate costume for me. I even had a sword. Stevie thought I looked stupid in the outfit. Some success.

I had two failures. First, I sucked my thumb, and Mrs. Nelson was determined to help me stop. She painted my thumb with blue ink, knowing that if I put it in my mouth, I would taste ink. After lunch the kids had nap time. I would lay on the mat and place my left arm in a way that I could in secret suck my thumb. I was busted following "nap time" since my face was covered in ink.

My second failure was more serious. My birthday is in October, so I was 5 when I entered first grade. I recall near the end of first grade the teacher gave us a test. I had no idea what it was about. It was as if I had been in a dream and there was no connection with prior events indicating where I was. I must have been in another world for six months of first grade. I suddenly felt that adult sense one feels when they are behind their contemporaries. The result was that my second-grade teacher wanted me to redo first grade.

My parents and their friends grew up in modest circumstances during the Great Depression and did not have the opportunity to enjoy eating beef often. As a result, good steaks were always on the menu at Lake Carroll. We were taught to eat T-bones with our hands so we could enjoy the aroma as much as the meal. Then we would sit around a fire, eat corn on the cob, and finish with my mother's pineapple upside-down cake.

We never had a problem with alligators. In the 1950s most of the gators had been killed. It was estimated that only 100,000 still lived in Florida versus 1.3 million today. Our only experience was once driving down the dirt side road to the lake house where we spotted an 8-footer strolling toward the lake. He was picked up by animal control.

My son Rowdy has a home on a Florida lake. He recently captured a six-foot gator in front of his house. He taped its mouth, tossed it in his truck and released it into the wild. He has a more challenging gator on a wild, ten-acre lake near his office. This beast is 13-15 feet long. Perhaps Florida needs to allow more gator kills?

Snakes were a different matter. Once my friend Benji Close picked up a pretty snake with orange and yellow coloring. He was not bitten, but it was a coral snake. Another time I was standing barefoot looking into the shallow water at a small stone wall two feet away and saw a two-inch-thick water moccasin squirming through the hole in the wall. Have you ever seen a startled cat jump? That was me. It scared me big time. It looked like a moray eel. My biggest fright was while fishing in a little pond a hundred yards from Lake Carroll. It had a 20-foot dock, and I was trying to catch some shell crackers. Across the pond a water moccasin saw me and headed right for me. This snake has a reputation for being aggressive, and he was after me. I ran like crazy to the club house. A week later, my sister Barbara had to go with me back to the pond to pick up some items I had left. I would not have gone back there alone.

The kids would run around barefoot playing hide and seek. How many children today have fathers they look up to and get to hang out with friends on a beautiful lake?

Sometimes during some weekends, we would drive out to Cypress Gardens and the ski show. My folks became friends with the owner Dick Pope. He loved the Air Force people. My mom could single ski on one foot backwards using her free foot to hold the rope. She participated in the portion of the show in which eight women were towed at the same time carrying flags. Then Colonel Don Hillman, Colonel Patrick Flemming and my father, now also a full colonel, were part of an act called "The Three Flying Colonels." They were a foil for the Cypress Gardens pros who could jump twice as far. First, the announcer would state over the microphone, "and here come the Three Flying Colonels." My father and his buddies would then fly over the jump. They would be followed by the "Garden's" pro jumpers. We had a lot of fun and were proud of our parents. I recall thinking that my dad could do anything.

Patrick Flemming was one of my father's best and most respected friends. During the war, Pat was the United States Navy's number four fighter ace with nineteen kills. He was lured from the Navy through the efforts of General Curtis LeMay to join the United States Air Force. Colonel Flemming flew Mach 1.2 in the Bell X-1 after Colonel Chuck Yeager broke the sound barrier in the aircraft. Patrick Flemming flew the B-47 with Colonel Don Hillman over the Siberian Region of the Soviet Union in secret reconnaissance missions. Colonel Flemming eventually became Deputy Wing Commander of the first B-52 wing. In a test mission, a fire broke out in his aircraft and Colonel Flemming's parachute caught fire as he attempted to bail out. His loss was a severe blow to the Strategic Air Command and the first crash of a B-52.

MacDill was a prime posting for combat pilots, while Lake Carroll was where officers and their families relaxed and socialized. My mother taught General Curtis LeMay to waterski there. LeMay later served as Chief of Staff of the Air Force under President Kennedy during the Cuban Missile Crisis. The colonel who wrote *12 O'clock High* visited, as did Colonel Paul Tibbets.

Jimmy Stewart, who flew combat missions out of England in World War II, starred in the movie *Strategic Air Command* filmed at MacDill. My father did the flying scenes in the B-47 for the movie. At the conclusion of the filming there was a party thrown at Lake Carroll. My grandfather and grandmother had been invited to join the group for the occasion. Jimmy commented to my dad that my grandfather, who was wearing shorts, was in heart failure. Colonel Stewart and later General Stewart pointed out that grandfather's legs were swollen which doctors call "Pedal Edema" I later learned. Stewart had seen these symptoms in a close friend. It turned out that the actor was correct.

That evening the Air Force had a more formal party to honor the movie's completion at the Officers' Club. My mother was Jimmy's "date" and had several dances with the actor. She had the habit of keeping many of her party dresses for years and this dress was no exception. Sixty years later in 2014 her granddaughter Monique Evans wore the dress to help her win the Miss Texas Beauty Pageant and then represent the state at the Miss America Pageant.

When I viewed the movie "Strategic Air Command" years later, I was surprised that it was nearly a direct reflection of my father and mother's experience up to that time. The exception was that the movie billboards emphasized the Convair ten-engine B-36 strategic bomber, the largest mass-produced piston-engine aircraft ever built, but was being phased out at the time. The movie depicts Lieutenant Colonel Jimmy Stewart as a baseball player drafted into the Air Force and assigned to SAC, due to the Korean War. The hero flew B-29 aircraft missions during World War II and thus was recalled to active duty. His wife played by June Allyson, is sad that her civilian life is upset but stands by her man. The

Commander of SAC, played by Frank Lovejoy, plays the role of General Curtis LeMay. Lovejoy even smoked a cigar in the movie that LeMay was known for. Stewart's character is named "Dutch" and visits or is stationed at four different air bases: MacDill, Carswell, Offutt, and Thule Greenland. Stewart learns to admire the mission of SAC as does the audience. Stewart soon becomes a "Bird" Full Colonel who practices midair refueling, a critical component of a mission requiring extended flight leads to Japan, Thule and MacDill. Stewart's arm is injured so that he cannot fly any longer in the B-47 and is allowed to leave the Air Force. He rejoins his baseball team as a coach since his hand is damaged.

My father was successful in the civilian world and due to his Korean War and prior experience, joined the Strategic Air Command. Richard Evans prior aircraft had been the B-29 flying missions over Japan and he was a Lieutenant Colonel. Like the movie character, Richard Evans soon became a Bird Colonel. My mother did not want to have her husband rejoin the Air Force but followed her husband. Richard Evans piloted the 35-hour jet refueling record which resulted in a multi-page article about this accomplishment and his crew's appearance on the cover of *Air Force* magazine's "10 Year Anniversary of SAC" issue. Like Stewart's character in the movie, Colonel Evans was stationed at Carswell, MacDill, Offutt and Thule Air Force Bases.

My father even had a broken arm, not injured flying or due to prior baseball excess. His arm was broken because of his crashing into the ski jump.

The Stewart character nickname of "Dutch" was coincidentally the nickname of Major Henry "Dutch" Deutschendorf. Major Deutschendorf was destined to hold several high-speed records while flying the Mach 2 B-58 in later years.

The following pages show Colonel Richard Evans and wife Jo Ann during that time. Granddaughter Monique Evans Isringhausen is shown wearing her grandmother's dress with my mom. It truly was a bueatiful 60-year-old dress.

Sometimes our parents would spend the Saturday with us at the lake and then take us back to the base. Then they would go back out to continue their party no longer in bathing suits but shorts and slacks on the men and dresses on the women.

My dad told me of one "Schadenfreude" joke the officers would pull on their wives. They would have the women barefoot and blindfolded. The men would take a few wet towels roll them and stretch them out in front of the women to form two lines. The towels were set at an angle to gradually stretch farther apart. The first victim would have to walk forward feeling the towel beneath her toes. Gradually the poor women would be barely able to stand upright as her legs were doing the splits. In the first round all the other women were in another room and unable to watch. After the first wife went through this procedure another officer, and not her husband, would lie on his back, looking up with his hands behind his head ten feet past the area she had struggled over in the splits.

Then they took off her blindfold. The lady was surrounded by laughing guys and at first did not realize what had happened. Nothing had happened, but she did not know that. When she turned around, she saw this man that apparently had been directly under her as she was doing the splits in her effort to shimmy over his body. He had a big smile. The reaction of the women was fury at the men and particularly at her husband for allowing her to be so embarrassed. Yet the men were innocent.

The fun started when the first woman was calmed down and joined the men to watch their next victim. As the process was repeated it was seen that the officer did not lay down between the towels until the women had passed by. The prior women then realized the trick the men were pulling. My father said the funny part was when you could see a lady anticipate her girlfriend's reaction.

All the wives were put through this ordeal to the delight of their husbands and all but the last victim.

I am aware of one non officer attending the Lake Carroll group. That was Sewart Mc Donald. He was an early barefoot skier. My father could barefoot but Stew was at another level of skill. Years later I would see a Vitalis Hair commercial on TV starring none other than "Barefoot Stew Mc Donald." Stew was always asking to borrow Don or my dad's boat.

General LeMay was an excellent mechanic and loved automobiles. For several years he would organize a race at MacDill. The enlisted men did not compete and apparently had to do extra work to prepare for the Auto Race Weekend. Some pulled a mild rebellion which resulted in a car disappearing. That ended the race.

LeMay had the reputation of being a very hard but a fair man. He knew that to have true professional military men serving in peace time, his troops had to be provided with better food, quality housing, superior sports facilities and higher pay. He worked hard to deliver these benefits for his first-class airmen and families. Remarkably, General LeMay was true "hands on the job" leader.

My mother shared a story about her experience at the hobby shop at Offutt Air Force Base. A heavy-set man without looking up asked if she would pass him a particular wrench as he worked on his car. She got him the wrench. It was Curtis LeMay, Four Star General and Commander of the Strategic Air Command.

I have not been to the Pentagon since childhood, but I am told that near the entrance is a sign that says, "What would LeMay do?" This reflects the widely held respect for the man. It was General LeMay that bravely led the Schweinfurt Raid by the 8th Air Force over Germany which resulted in a 49 percent attrition rate of the B-17 aircraft. After departing Europe for the Pacific Theatre, he organized the Tinian firebombing raids over Japan. He directed the dropping of the atomic bombs as directed by Truman and Forrestal. He oversaw the Berlin Airlift. LeMay literally conceived, built, and commanded what is arguably the most effective deterrent force in the world following World War II, the Strategic Air Command. He was Chief of Staff of the United States Air Force during the Cuban missile crisis. His leadership and unique ideas place him in the same league as Stonewall Jackson. My father had the greatest respect for his superior General LeMay.

Sometimes traveling around Florida, I saw a chain gang. There were white and black men chained, I believe by the legs, moving down the highway chopping weeds. I do not know why but I found this site frightening. The movie *Cool Hand Luke* got that scene right.

I recall seeing black people in Florida. What stands out in my mind is the recollection of the drinking fountains. There was a white one and a black one. My mother explained the difference and told me how wrong the policy was. The effect it had on me was to think that the white fountain was cleaner than the black. It was probably taken better care of by the Florida State government. There is no doubt that separating the races in this manner enforced a prejudice of white people versus black people and was very wrong.

The military services lead the country as they were integrated in 1949, so we did not see the racism of the civilian world very much. I interacted with several black military people in my life. One summer prior to going to college, I worked with four black boys my age loading farm equipment on trucks in Fort Worth, Texas. When we had our lunch over a coke and a couple of chili dogs, I realized that the odds were high that my life was going to be better than theirs. They simply were not afforded the advantage of "knowing the game" and how to play it. My Air Force Basic Training Instructor was black. One day while he was out of the barracks I snuck into his office and put on his extra hat. You know the ones they would cock to one side to add to their image as an overlord while they callously yelled at you. My buddy Toni Vulin took the picture of me with my feet on the TI's desk wearing the TI's hat. I thought I was very daring at the time. I am beyond glad the TI did not catch us. I have only known fine patriotic black men in the military.

Richard Evans took our family on a vacation trip to the Florida Keys traveling along the main highway known as Alligator Alley prior to the modern freeway. It must have been a Sunday because I saw numerous black families by a canal fishing. They were using cane poles with line tied to the very end. The women wore clean, white, long dresses and white turbans. Their families looked very nice. As I travel through an airport today and observe the way most Americans dress it is a bit sad. I am not the exception. Americans 70 years ago, in my judgement, took more pride in their appearance.

Birth of a SAC Brat

SAC Brat in his Gasparilla parade pirate costume

Five tom cats, Colonel Don Hillman second from left

Colonel Mike McCoy and General Curtis LeMay discussing planned 35-hour record attempt

Colonel Mike McCoy and Lt Colonel Richard Evans planning the B-47 35-hour mid-air refueling record attempt

Lt Colonel Richard Evans being congratulated for setting the 35-hour refueling record

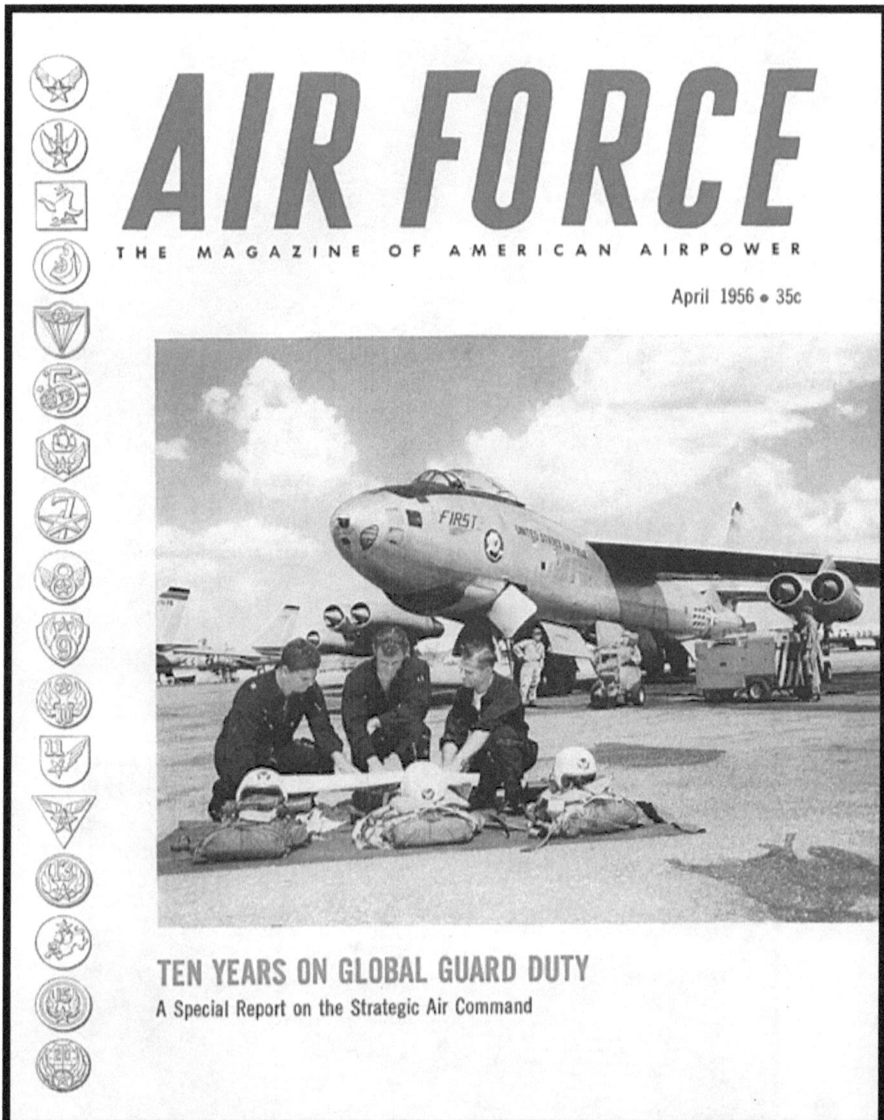

AIR FORCE

THE MAGAZINE OF AMERICAN AIRPOWER

April 1956 • 35c

TEN YEARS ON GLOBAL GUARD DUTY

A Special Report on the Strategic Air Command

Air Force Magazine, April 1956: "Ten Years on Global Guard Duty" — a special report on the Strategic Air Command documenting the setting of the mid-air refueling record

The three "flying Colonels" at Cypress Gardens ski show: Don Hillman, Richard Evans, and Pat Flemming

Jo Ann and Richard Evans water skiing at Cypress Gardens

Colonel Don Hillman, Lloyd Hillman, Jo Ann Evans, and Colonel Richard Evans at Cypress Gardens

Evans family at Lake Carroll

Jo Ann Evans in party dress for the movie Strategic Air Command

Monique Evans in her grandmother's "party dress" with her grandmother, Jo Ann

Saxon "Rowdy", Don, Machelle, and Monique Evans

Lt Colonel Richard Evans

Chapter 14: Growing Up at Offutt

The stress on families was great. My father was sent to Thule, Greenland and England for six months. When he returned, we were transferred to Offutt Air Force Base, Bellevue, Nebraska. That was SAC headquarters. My mother did not want to go to Nebraska. She eventually took my sister and me to her childhood home in San Antonio, Texas. It was said that a higher-than-normal percent of SAC families ended up in divorce and my mother wanted a divorce.

In the summer of 1955, my sister and I were living with our grandparents and our mother. That September, I was put into the Woodlawn Elementary School and the second-grade teacher wanted to put me back into the first grade. There was no Gasparilla Parade to bail me out. Coincidentally, the same teacher had taught my mother in first grade and had wanted to put her back a year. The educator must have thought our family was stupid and I was carrying on the tradition.

My parents reconciled in time for me to escape from the clutches of that teacher to the safety of SAC headquarters and a Bellevue, Nebraska school. My mother worked diligently to help me catch up. In half a year. I was doing fine.

The SAC Brats would naturally move with their fathers to the new assignment, usually staying at new locals three to four years. Since our fathers often worked together at a prior base, the Brats often ended up at new bases with many of their old friends. Thus Stevie Hillman, Freddie Leonard, Burt Trimble, Richard (Dick) Wear, and Joe Yahr were my main friends. Being a SAC brat meant leaving friends as well and having to make new ones. We learned that moving lets you challenge yourself and connect with new people. I think that any military service Brat on average is superior to civilians at meeting new people and making friends. You had to learn.

If I oversaw a sales department, I would tend to hire military children over civilians because the Brats on average were more respectful, more worldly and more outgoing. The danger of an employer hiring a grown-up Brat was that the Brat would get bored after a few years and transfer to a new job. The Brat was a greater risk of learning the business and then going out on their own to compete. SAC Brats, raised in the disciplined environment of an Air Force Base surprisingly developed more independent personalities.

A wonderful example of a military Brat's independent nature was the story of how Kris Kristofferson met the country-western singer Johnny Cash. Unable to secure a meeting to have Cash view some of his songs, Kristofferson determined when Cash was at home and then piloted a helicopter onto Johnny Cash's mansion front lawn.

The Brats called Offutt Air Force Base "Awful Air Force Base". It was likely due to the tough Nebraska winters, but I enjoyed the base. The name might have stuck just because it was so close and kids can be smart alecs.

Offutt had quite a history. It had been used as a manufacturing location to build 531 B-29 bombers. There was an officer's row of large Victorian houses near the parade ground in which many American generals lived over the years. There was a movie theatre nearby. On the North side of the base there was a huge building that was used to manufacture the two B-29's that dropped the atomic bombs on Japan. I recall a bowling alley and a workout center there.

We lived in Wary Housing which was on the north side of the base with a small road to the base fence. I could walk a hundred yards up the road, go by the fence, and then drop down the sidewalk on the other side to Bellevue Elementary School. While Offutt was the center of SAC, I never saw a guard on that road or near that fence. I assume it was watched by security, but I never saw the watchers. I also knew of ways to get into MacDill and later Carswell Air Force Bases.

I recall the movie *Iron Eagle* in which the military Brats assisted by a black officer plan an air operation to save one of the boy's fathers. The Air Force Brats in the movie reminded me of my friends at the air bases. Because we were not adults, we were able to get away with sneaking or exploring various aspects of the bases we lived on. I am sure security kept an eye on us and we were not aware, but we did "get around."

We would ride our sleds down Radar Hill. We would gather treasures from the dumpster behind the base exchange. We could get a coke for five cents; a mounds candy bar was ten cents, and we could view the magazine counter at our leisure. There were some very strange magazines at those counters that I never saw in a civilian store. The cover would have a bunch of Nazi's, dressed in uniforms and swastika armbands surrounded by good looking German women with fighting going on around them. Inside there would be some silly fictional story. Someone should have told the editor that the war ended ten years earlier and now the Germans were our buddies.

General LeMay wanted his pilots to be trained in martial arts. My dad took classes every Saturday and there was a class for the Brats. LeMay likely did this to assist in escape and evasive awareness for pilots shot down or perhaps to instill a greater martial spirit with the troops. My father had a side arm for his flights as well. I recall fondly fighting with my father after each of our judo lessons. When I swept his foot, he would occasionally act like I tripped him and would fall to the mat. Everyone has seen in a movie how the hero uses the villain's weight to roll backward and the bad guy flies over the top. The first move is to push your opponent. When he pushes back you pull him over the top. My father would play along using this move and I would roll backwards as he flew across the room. This was simply hilarious for a 7-year-old boy.

I cannot emphasize enough the mobilized culture that LeMay developed. He wanted his forces to go to war in minutes. The strain must have been terrible for our fathers and mothers. As their children, we did not feel this pressure but felt proud of our fathers. I recall once my father told me about a dream he had. He said that he woke up with his fingers laced behind his head and his fingers feeling a lot of pain. What had occurred was that he had fallen asleep with his hands and fingers clasped together behind his head. In the dream he thought he was a prisoner of war, and his hands were bound in that manner. He told me how he pulled and pulled in his sleep to get his hands separated to get free and escape and thus the finger injury.

On summer weekends we would go south along the Platte River to a sandy lake and water ski. I had a blow-up kayak my father purchased for me on one of his trips to England. Dick Wear and I had a blast going all over the lake on our own. At night we would have the traditional steak dinner and my mom's upside-down cake.

One night by the fire I noticed a piece of wood with one end in the slightly burning ashes and the other upright. With a piece of wood as a fulcrum, it looked like a teeter-totter. I got the bright idea of jumping on the higher end and expecting the portion under the ashes to pop up like a little explosion. Young boys and particularly SAC Brats think like that. I jumped as high as I could and landed on my right foot hitting the wood perfectly. Sure enough, the other side popped up with the ash explosion. My problem was that the piece of wood that I put all my weight on had a six-inch nail in it.

I screamed in pain as the nail went through my heel and out just below my ankle. My father came over and tried to pull out the nail. He was a strong man but could not pull it out. After great effort he removed the nail. It did not bleed much and there was far less pain, but I recovered by laying on a blanket by the fire like a whimpering dog.

It is hard to describe the respect that we had for our parents and particularly our fathers. Part of it was the time in American history. Part of it was that we tended to be from southern families and manners were important. Part of it was the Air Force culture in which as the sun went down so did the flag, the anthem was played, and everyone stopped what they were doing showing their respect.

There was a TV show at the time called *Sky King*. Sky would always get himself into a fix and then bravely used his airplane to win the day. Our dads were more courageous than Sky King. You could ask a civilian kid, "What does your father do?" "Why, he sells real estate." A civilian asks a SAC Brat in 1956 at the height of the Cold War, "What does your dad do?" Answer: "He flies at 1000 miles an hour to train so that the Russians do not destroy our civilization."

I recall returning from the lake at night several times half sleeping. My sister Barbara was four years older so she could not get away with my game. I would sometimes be carried from the car to bed by our father to avoid being awakened. In my case, I was awake but appreciated the love of my parents. I was not going to miss out on having my dad tuck me in. A funny thing about the SAC brats was that while we lived on air bases that were likely the first targets in a nuclear attack on our country, our parents made us feel loved and safe.

My mother tended to be more financially responsible than my father. My father was an idealistic man that loved the Air Force mission and its people. He practiced his personal life with bravery. He lived for the moment. My mother thought more about the future. Mom persuaded my father to move off base and invest in a home in Bellevue. I learned at Bellevue Elementary School that "Bellevue" meant in French "beautiful view." I never saw a view, but it was a great place for kids.

Our house was a quarter of a mile from my new school and a mile from the air base. There was a cornfield and hay field that met at the back of the property. SAC brats were everywhere. We could play in the cornfields and catch snakes and build forts out of the bales of hay. There was an old French mission that gave the locale the name Mission Heights. We'd camp out, build tree swings and forts under the ground using scrap wood as roofs from the many suburban building sites in the area. In keeping with our Air Force mission our home was a block from a road named LeMay Way.

The boys used to enjoy crawling through long storm drains without flashlights. I am not referring to the large stand-up ones but the drains that a small animal or a seven-or eight-year-old child can crawl through. The concrete drainpipes would have a slight decline. I recall a few times crawling through a hundred yards or more in the cement enclosure while alone. I would reach a point at which it was entirely dark. There never were any animal noises, or I would have been frightened. I knew that the drain had an exit, so I pressed forward crawling on my jeans covered knees feeling the cobwebs brush my face. The bottom of the storm drain was clean to the toach of my hands as they reached forward into the blackness. I never ran into a rat, a snake or the bones of a dead animal as I crawled forward. Finally, I would see the proverbial light at the end of the tunnel and work my way out. I told my father years later about this activity and he told me he was horrified.

I retold this story years later to my children to explain the process that I guess a young person goes through to find reward, purpose and success. When we are young, we are told by those we respect to move forward, study hard, and work hard. We blindly accept this advice because we are told there is a reward at the end of the tunnel. If we are fortunate the source of our advice is from a respected person that loves us.

I recall in my teens when thinking about my future that all the potential opportunities for success were taken. Someone discovered how to build a car and an airplane. All the gold had been mined. All the treasure in the sea had been discovered and put into museums. What was left for me? I learned that nature is constantly changing and opportunities appear. When a bird wakes in the morning, he has no idea where its next meal will come from but usually nature provides.

I told my kids that they must have the courage to go into the dark tunnel. They must work as hard as they can and believe they can get through the tunnel to their reward. There may be the sounds of frightening animals near their hands as they crawl forward in the darkness, but nature will provide. There are riches and fulfilled dreams in the tunnel for those that believe and will not give up.

Having a mentor is so important as we grow into adulthood. Trust in that mentor allows us to move forward without seeing the reward. A mentor allows us to take steps that we sense will help our future and yet frighten us. A great example would be overcoming the fear of public speaking. Ralph Waldo Emerson said, "Do the thing we fear, and the death of fear is certain." The greatest success, growth and pride of accomplishment come from living outside one's fractal or comfort zone. The men of the Strategic Air Command said it another way "No guts, No Glory."

SAC Brats were surrounded by excellent mentors encouraging youngsters to strive outside their comfort zone. Europe in the 15th century lived outside its comfort zone and the result was centuries of success.

It is tragic that many American children grow up without a father present. A loving nurturing mother is less likely to encourage her children to take the prudent risks and to live outside their comfort zone. A loving father is likely the best mentor for a boy and possibly a girl. Men that abandon their children and thus remove a loving mentor are beyond despicable for they greatly reduce their children's chance for a happy life.

My father used to use surfing as analogous to success. Two people try to catch the same wave. One paddles his heart out and slides into the wave. The rider then rides through an effortless experience. The other surfer does not paddle as hard at the start. He gets to the edge or lip of the wave but cannot quite drop in. He spends his life struggling at the edge. The lesson is that hard work early in life can result in not having to work as hard as others for the remainder of life to achieve freedom and success.

Unfortunately, so many of our children lack proper mentors. Matters are made worse because some of our politicians and the media tell segments of our population that the reason their parents and they are not successful is the view that the system is against them. The media in some cases is almost raising our children. The media does not love them as parents do. The media wants them to obey and buy often useless products. The media wants these youngsters to grow up to be slaves. The politician flatters the ignorant and lies to get their vote.

When a young person living in America buys into the victimhood argument they are doomed. When a young person senses they are behind their contemporaries in the competitive race we humans thrive in, they have a choice. They can run from the tunnel and blame other people, or they can strive and push outside their comfort zone. There is no guarantee that living a more courageous life will promise success. It is guaranteed to increase your odds and that makes life a fair game.

I respected more than feared my father. I recall two times when I really got into trouble. The first time I was in fourth grade. I showed my father how you could take a bobby pin and a rubber band and make a sling shot in your hand. I was able to shoot the bobby pin at a pretty good distance. My father told me to never shoot anyone with my invention. A week later I was looking down on our laundry chute and there was my sister Barbara. I could not resist and shot her with the bobby pin. I barely missed her eye and she screamed in pain. This resulted in a major spanking, and my father was mad at me. He then gave me the paddle and ordered me to whack him a few times. My father believed in the adage, "this is hurting me more than you, son."

I do not recall the specifics of the other time or two, but those punishments were almost done in a humorous manner. I knew that I had done something wrong. I would pay the penalty, there was no anger, and the message would be brief. No hurt feelings but necessary to bring the young Brat back into line. My father had a paddle board which doubled as a SAC Brat trainer. It was oversized and had numerous even spaced holes in it. My father used to joke that the key to using the paddleboard was by employing your wrist to as he said "follow through" on the stroke. I recall a few times when I was to get a whack or two and he joked about how spankings were the same way. The key to a good spanking was to follow through using your wrist. I recall laughing at this gallows humor.

I think the nature of men that have experienced hardship due to combat is to unconsciously use humor to compensate during fearful moments and despair to manage the situation. My father told me how he saw a British Lancaster bomber crash and burst into flames. Fortunately, the entire crew got out prior to the fire. My father commented to the pilot about the close call. The pilot's answer was "piece of cake" British for "no big deal". My dear friend Burt Trimble was killed in a freak landslide due to rain in San Diego in 1969. Burt managed to push his girlfriend out of the way, saving her life.

A few months later, Burt's father, Colonel Harry Trimble, visited my father and me at our home in Palos Verdes. I naturally told Colonel Trimble how sorry I was for the loss of my friend and his 19-year-old and only son. Harry said almost casually, "Old Burt had to get himself killed."

Colonel Trimble was over 40, flew combat missions in World War Two and Korea. He trained Republic F-105 Thunderchief fighter-bomber pilots at George Air Force Base near Mojave, California. Colonel Trimble volunteered to go to Vietnam to fly highly dangerous bombing missions in the F-105. That is the way he delt with the grief of the loss of his wonderful son.

The men of the Strategic Air Command through their example taught me that laughter and humor can help get people through tough situations.

While I enjoyed family weekends at the lake with swimming, kayaking, fishing and water skiing, it seemed that I could not learn to water ski. My sister Barbara could. My father tried to teach me, but I either did not have leg strength or convinced myself that I could not do it. Instead, my father taught me how to get up on double skis with him. I would place my feet in front of his and my arms inside his with my hands on the rope handle. We would yell "hit it" and up we jumped. He soon taught me to step forward on the skis, and he would bend his head down. I would then climb on his back and sit on his shoulders. Then my father would drop one ski, so we were single skiing with me on his shoulders. Years later I developed the skill to do this routine with my kids though not on the single ski.

I first learned to water ski during the summer after fourth grade. Colonel Trimble took me out to the lake with Burt, who could ski, and worked with me. My father suspected that I was unable to ski due to the pressure of my parents being very good at the sport, and I may have felt a bit intimidated. It was the combination of Colonel Trimble's patience with Burt's encouragement that I was off and flying. I soon learned slalom with Burt's leadership.

Burt Trimble, as a son, would make any father proud. Burt was a handsome, athletic, and well-rounded person. Always kind and polite but under this gentleman was a strong leader. I used to enjoy diving, but Burt rarely dived. I recall his visiting us and the fathers and sons goofing around in the back yard pool on my father's dura flex diving board.

There was light competition between Burt and me as our fathers enjoyed a beer as they watched. I developed the ability to do the typical noncompetitive dives like a one and a half or a two or one and a half gainer. These were standard air base pool high dives in which I'd get lots of height with little form. My diving buddies and I would show up at the officers' club pool and do our routine to announce our presence. The finale was a massive watermelon next to the lifeguard station.

After being forced to sit out of the pool for 20 minutes, we could then swim.

Burt was too much of a gentleman to act in this way, but he could do a few dives. In our backyard competition, I would perform some of my moves, typical dives that took many tries to learn. Since the failures could be painful as I hit the water, I would often wait seconds longer than necessary on the diving board to build up my courage to attempt the new dive. Burt would follow me and would not hesitate to build his courage. He would attack the dive. The next time Burt would hit the dive. Burt just did the dive almost perfectly. I recall how all four of us kept laughing as Burt progressed through the dives.

When my family was stationed at Carswell Air Force Base, Burt and I were ten years old. I remember visiting his home which was located a mile from the base. We were fishing off the bank of the Trinity River. Some old man had caught a 5 lb. turtle. I do not think it was even a snapping turtle. The turtle was scared and ducked its head into its shell, but this man shoved a knife into the spot into the poor turtle's head. I was horrified by the cruelty. I looked over at Burt and he was in tears. He was not bawling but had tears in his eyes.

With all the bone-headed young men in the world, why did we lose Burt Trimble?

Dick Wear lived across the street from us in Mission Heights. His father had transferred to SAC headquarters from Guam. I remember him telling me about Japanese soldiers still refusing to surrender and hiding in the "Boondocks" in Guam. This was nine years after the Pacific War had concluded. I was not surprised to learn years later of a Japanese soldier surrendering decades after the war's end.

Note the nature of the conversations between SAC Brats versus the civilian kids. The SAC kids were aware of geography and world conflicts while most of the civilian kids might know about a famous baseball player. The children of SAC airmen were generally aware of the great world struggle going on while the civilian kids had little idea.

Dick's room was full of airplane models, spaceship models and war plane posters. The SAC Brats could name every United States aircraft going back many years. They knew the airplane's speed and range. Often their fathers flew the aircraft. Every SAC Brat boy knew what the Revelle Company did. Boeing, Convair and North American Aviation were household words.

Dick and I would often play on the farmer's property behind my house. One time we captured a four-foot bull snake and showed it to my mother. Dick expected her to run but mom just picked up the snake. She was a San Antonio, Texas girl who used to enjoy floating down the San Antonio River during the summer with friends catching snakes in the overhanging trees. I recall Dick, after witnessing my mother passing the snake test saying, "your mom is so cool." You know, she was. Mom must have passed the snake gene to Monique. During her year as Miss Texas, Monique hosted the "Rattle Snake Roundup" in Sweetwater. Mo had to walk in hip-high leather boots through 1,200 ankle-deep hissing rattle snakes. She then had to help milk one for venom. They kept that snake almost refrigerated to keep it from biting her. One of the handlers was bitten and had to go to the hospital.

On the non-lake weekends the kids would go to Judo school and then hang out at the base movie theatre. The movie cost 19 cents. If we did not have a ride, we had to walk from the B-29 factory building area where Judo was taught on the north side of Offutt along the runway fence to the west. I recall looking up on the west end of that runway and seeing giant aircraft take off right over our heads. The ground seemed to shake as the plane passed over. We would then walk along the fence back to the east and make a right or southern turn toward the old Victoria homes and the movie theatre area.

Some of the Saturday movies had ongoing adventures in which the hero would get into an impossible situation only to get saved the next weakened. Most of what we watched were western movies. When the movie ended, the boys would be so fired up that we would come running out on the grass and pretend we were shooting one another and seeing who could make the most realistic fall.

Sometimes we would just walk past the guard gate unchallenged right into Offutt Air Force Base, the nerve center of America's nuclear might. But we were just Brats.

Halloween at Offutt Air Force Base was a blast. General LeMay made great efforts to provide reasonable housing for his men and their families, but money was short. The housing for the airmen was like large apartments. Most officers' quarters were not much bigger. Unlike in a suburb, the distances between each home were small. The result was very efficient candy harvesting for the Trick or Treaters. We would stay out until 9:00 PM and load up. One time my mother and her modeling girlfriend Toni Leanord snuck up on my sister and me. Mom had this gorilla mask on and said, "what are you doing little boy?" She was right next to me and I was startled. She was 29 then. She never took herself too seriously and had a wonderful sense of humor.

After Stevie and Burt's parents were transferred, my best friend was Dick Wear. He would sometime go to the lake with our group. One time we found some wood and nails up the beach and built a raft. We even had a small sail. We boarded our raft and it got windy. We ended up on the other side of the lake. It was no big deal when my father picked us up at the end of the day.

Another time the officers were skiing and the boat shut down. The engine restarted easily but it was impossible to get the boat into gear. The officers opened the engine cover and looked at the gearing mechanism. Some of these pilots had engineering degrees and knew engines. One of the Brats suggested that the propeller had fallen off. The pilots initially laughed and ignored the suggestion and continued their investigation. A minute later they looked at each other with a grin and an expression that said, "maybe the kid is right". Sure enough, the prop had spun off.

Years later I was traveling across the USA with my young son, Hunter. We stopped at the Bellagio Hotel. We were pulling a small trailer and decided to park in the basement. After traveling 50 feet the roof of the trailer hit the ceiling of the basement and got stuck. I could not move the car or trailer. I visualized a heavy-set tow operator with a cigar and a pit bull in the cab telling me how expensive it would be to remove that trailer. Then young Hunter suggested I reduce the air in the tires. You can see why I had trouble in first grade.

I cannot possibly understand the pressure on the pilots of the Strategic Air Command. Periodically one of them would die in an accident in a high-performance aircraft.

There were air crews always on alert. If ordered they had twelve minutes to drive out on the runway, starting their aircraft, and perhaps 15-20 large aircraft would be attempting to take off clearing the field.

They knew that if they did not travel many miles from their base their aircraft might be destroyed by the nuclear blast hitting their air base. These pilots also knew that they had three options in their future. First, they could get shot down by Soviet defenses. Second, they could have a successful attack on the Soviet Union and land on a friendly base or even an interstate highway. Third, they might be able to bail out of their aircraft and survive. They also know as they flew toward the Russian homeland that their sole purpose of deterring war had failed.

Lastly, these men would know as they left their bases that those friends and loved ones remaining would likely be dead in minutes. Numerous nuclear weapons would be used to assure the bases were destroyed. The result would be almost a guarantee that their wives and children would be killed even if the pilots survived. People living in big cities might have time to evacuate if the Russian attempt was a "First Strike" to destroy the United States nuclear deterrence. One theory was to launch a First Strike and avoid the cities. Afterwards the opponent could use nuclear blackmail to negotiate terms.

There were no bomb shelters for the SAC families to hide in and no time to use them if war came.

I suspect that increased alcohol consumption was in part due to the pressure. One night one of my father's friends had a few drinks and decided to show several Omaha journalists the B-52. He guided his group out to the flight line and approached a sentry guarding one of the aircraft. I do not know if the B-52 was ready alert to ferry nuclear weapons to the Soviet Union. This pilot had no business taking civilians out to visit the airplane particularly at night.

The armed guard insisted that the pilot and journalists not board the aircraft. Apparently, a confrontation occurred resulting in the guard being bullied into backing down by the higher-ranking officer. The journalist got their tour of the airplane. Unfortunately for the pilot, not only did the guard report the incident, but local newspapers also reported the incident. Soon my father's buddy had a new assignment on an Air Base in Alaska.

In another incident my father and a pilot colleague were taking off in a Lockheed T-33 Shooting Star to Andrews Air Force base near

Washington and the Pentagon. Colonel Evans was in the back seat of the two-place single engine jet. The pilot accelerated the aircraft down the runway. Prior to lifting off and becoming airborne, he retracted the landing gears. The result of this reckless "stunt" would be a sharp lift off the runway as the air resistance to the aileron and tires was removed.

During this takeoff the pilot raised the landing gear prior to getting positive lift and the aircraft did not rise but started to drop. Another foot or two and the pilot, my father and the T-33 loaded with jet fuel would have been a fireball. Though the pilot was a fine officer and out ranked my father, my father told him to never do that again or he would be reported.

The stakes and pressure were very high on these brave men. Reckless efforts to relieve pressure or generate some excitement could go wrong and the rewards could be an unwanted tour in Alaska or even death.

I remember 1956 clearly. My father had a revolutionary stereo system. We laughed at Tom Leher's *Hunting Song* and marveled at the *1812 Overture* with real cannon blasting at the climax.

The shock in 1957 was Sputnik. The Russians while lagging far behind SAC in offensive bombing capability had developed a lead in missile technology. I remember one late night getting up and walking into our living room and my father was studying some "top secret" slides on his screen. I asked him what was going on.

Colonel Richard Evans elevated responsibility at SAC Headquarters was to chair a committee that studied new weapons system for SAC then presented recommendations to SAC Commander Curtis LeMay. Two weapons systems selected to sustain the future SAC mission over the next 20 years, were under consideration. The first was the B-58 "Hustler" bomber, an aircraft that could sprint at speeds up to 1,300 miles per hour or Mach 2. The B-58 would be designed to obtain a range of 3,000 miles so it like the B-47 would have to be refueled midair to achieve its mission of attacking Soviet Russia.

The second aircraft was to be the B-70. This airplane was programed to fly at 2100 miles per hour or Mach 3. It required titanium structural components since the temperature generated by Mac 3 flight speed would melt a typical aluminum wing.

There was a contest to name the B-70. Being partially of Norwegian ancestry I always thought this beautiful airplane was given a beautiful name, the Valkyrie. The Norse demigoddess flew over a battlefield and retrieved the dead heroes to Valhalla. To this day I love Wagners' "Ride of the Valkyrie." It forces the listener to experience the spiritual and exciting side of war ignoring the tragedy and blood.

My father told me that the Soviet Union might have a strategic lead over my country and my country might be in trouble if we did not catch up. In Europe the Hungarians, who had fought the Russians in World War II and were occupied by the Russian Army, were in revolt. I did not know as a child that the Soviet Union had reasons to fear us and Western Europe. Europeans had invaded Russia multiple times resulting in millions of civilians and soldiers' deaths.

The Soviet Union's leaders feared the Hungarians would join the West and then perhaps Poland and other states controlled by Russia would do the same. The Soviet Red Army moved into Hungary and in a bloody manner ended the revolt. Many in the United States thought we should join the Hungarians and fight the Russians. Our leaders wisely understood that Russia would do almost anything to protect this region from becoming a future enemy of Russia. Doesn't Russia feel the same about the Ukraine in our time? As in 1956, is the United States in any better position to help the Ukrainians 5,000 miles from our borders?

The Egyptians in 1956 decided to nationalize the Suez Canal. Geographically the entire canal runs through Egyptian territory, but French and British built it so they controlled the canal. Note the growing trend of former colonies asserting their power over former mother countries was developing.

In a lightning move, the British, French and Israelis attacked the Egyptians driving them from the canal. The militarily-dominate United States did not approve of the controversial move against Egypt, the occupation withdrew, and control of the canal reverted to the Egyptians where it remains today. At this juncture, French and English were affectively not potent powers east of the Suez Canal. The America and Russia became competing geopolitical powers in the Persian Gulf and Middle East.

"Nothing is new under the sun." Note how seven decades later, the Unite States Congress' Armed Services and Appropriations Committees fail to agree on the degree to which an eastern European nation should be supported while selected United States elected leaders perceive Russian national interests to be at stake. In this instance, the European NATO countries, who have shirked financial NATO contributions across several decades find themselves dependent on the United States' power. As these European countries express growing concern regarding the Russian invasion of Ukaraine, the United States Executive and Legislative branches are reluctant to enter the fray, while the Europeans lack the ability to respond effectively. We are also witnessing a war in another chokepoint of the Middle East. The Germans, French and British governments, who are deficient in geographical power as validated by their diminished military powers, resign themselves as bystanders. In this case, the French and British are now more dependent on United States power and having been told by the United States that the United States is in charge, are reluctant to participate or help.

My father told me he believed the Soviet Union would soon have an effective ICBM strike capability and that it was imperative that our country close the gap. This development was the beginning of a trough for the manned airpower component of a SAC built around the manned bomber with missiles as a secondary mission. Initially, to prolong its existence, increase flexibility and allow a "standoff" attack capability, SAC developed the Snark and Hound dog missiles. These weapons allowed a SAC bomber to launch an attack outside the range of the Soviet air defenses. These weapons were essentially modernized versions of the German V-1's or buzz bombs used against England during the war. Their maximum speeds were around 600 miles per hour.

As the Strategic Air Command responded to the ICBM threat, funding shifted from procuring manned bombers to the nation's ground-based nuclear deterrent, which produced a progression of expensive strategic ballistic missiles including the Atlas, Titan, Jupiter, Minutemen I, II, and III, and the ten-warhead Peacekeeper that remains on alert today.

In the interim, the strategic bomber component of SAC has been reduced to 19 B-2 stealth bombers combined with 40 B-1B Lancer supersonic, variable sweep-wing, strategic bomber introduced in the late 1980s. The B-1s, were targeted for retirement, but the entire fleet has undergone life-extension upgrade and will remain in active service until fully replaced by the next-generation B-21 Raider strategic bomber in the 2030s. Seventy-six upgraded Boeing B-52H Stratofortress bombers will remain in service until at least 2050, when the youngest aircraft will be 88 years old. The United States is finally attempting to dig out of the bomber trough with the introduction of the B-21 Raider Long Range Strike-Bomber, the world's first, sixth generation combat aircraft that can hold at risk, any target on the face of the Earth according to the Air Force. The Program of Record calls to produce 100 or more of the highly stealthy bombers that integrate advanced artificial intelligence, computer networking and data fusion while employing Collaborative Combat Aircraft.

I learned more about geopolitical issues as a fifth grader. I could not understand why, during World War II our enemies, and therefore the bad people, were the Germans, Italians and Japanese. The good people were the British, French, Russians, Canadians, Australians, and Chinese. The Swedes and Spanish had been moderately bad for helping the Germans. Ten years after the war ended, the Russians and Chinese which had been good, were bad. The Germans, Italians and Japanese which had been very evil, were now good. The Swedes and Spanish had become better.

The reader may laugh and think that it is nonsense for me to argue that I thought about these issues at such a young age. My level of exposure and rare vantage point to the leadership at the Strategic Air Command allowed me to listen and to think about these issues. Several of my SAC Brat friends did as well. This was somewhat confusing but the constant dialogue by SAC seniors whetted my interest. I did understand that my country had friends in Western Europe and particularly England and that SAC was the powerful force that kept the Soviet Union from conquering Europe and England.

The SAC Brats in front of Wary Housing in Offutt Air Force Base

Boeing B-52 Stratofortress

The darker side of Jo Ann Evans, Halloween 1956

Chapter 15: Command of the B-58 Test Program

My father, who was a civilian and an active-duty Air Force Reservist from 1946 to 1951, understandably fell behind promotionally compared to his contemporaries that had remained on active duty. It was therefore a singular turning point that in 1956 Colonel Evans earned professional recognition with an opportunity that offered him the potential to become a General Officer. General LeMay, Commander of the Strategic Air Command (SAC) hand-picked Richard Evans to be the first Air Force Officer to fly the new B-58. My father was presented with the honor of leading the Air Force's test program for what was to be the first supersonic bomber in the world.

The fact that Colonel Evans had extensive experience in dealing with British leadership and held the refueling record likely helped him win the job. The B-58 like the B-47 would require midair refueling to strike the Soviet Union and return.

The first step for Richard Evans was to learn to fly or "get checked out" in a supersonic aircraft. While the T-38 was the aircraft used by the Air Force for this training, my father trained in the Convair F-102 Delta Dagger, the Air Force's first operational supersonic fighter interceptor. This aircraft was delta winged like the B-58 with some of the same flying characteristics. Its maximum speed was ten or fifteen miles per hour faster than a B-58.

My father told me of a serious mistake that he made while flying the F-102. These aircraft had what was known as afterburners. This portion of the jet engine allowed the burning of excess jet fuel thus providing a jolt of excess power to the engine. It was common to kick in the afterburner on an engine when a pilot was starting his takeoff roll in the rush to achieve the desired altitude. The activity also burned a lot more fuel, so afterburner usage was not at cruising speed.

Colonel Evans was adjusting to flying the F-102 and apparently gaining some confidence. Perhaps too much confidence. My father took his F-102 into a vertical rise and then rolled it over to complete a loop. As he headed into the downside portion of the loop he had forgotten to turn off his afterburner. He was traveling at full speed toward the ground driven by gravity and his engine. Realizing his error, my father shut down the afterburner and pulled his aircraft out of the dive. He was experiencing considerable g (gravity) forces and at risk of blacking out as blood was rushing out of his head to other parts of his body caused by the deceleration of the aircraft. My dad said that he could hear bolts holding his wings and aircraft body together popping due to the force.

Meanwhile somewhere in the U. S. a child was walking to school, a plumber was fixing a stopped-up drain, and a woman was going shopping. These good people had no knowledge of the various drama going on in the sky above them playing out by people earning government salaries, risking their lives to protect their fellow Americans.

In World War II the famed German Stuka Dive bomber and American Naval dive bombers had dive brakes designed to slow down the aircraft during dive bombing and thus reducing the g forces the pilots had to endure. Often the g-forces forcing blood from the brain would cause the pilot to black out for a few seconds, a condition later diagnosed as G-force induced loss of consciousness or G-LOCK. Personal flight equipment, including G suits, was designed to help the pilot adapt to this life-threatening challenge. The aircraft had equipment to adjust to this problem.

Colonel Evans's F-102 was a fighter interceptor and did not have the advantage of a dive brake. Stuka pilots were not burdened with the unbridled power of an after-burner. Multiple Air Force and Navy supersonic fighter pilots fatally impacted the ground in broad daylight for what was believed to be unexplained reasons. After extensive flight surgeon research, it was determined the unexplained cause was, in fact, G-LOC, so my father was fortunate to have not completely blacked out and to have lived through that experience. When he returned to the base, Colonel Evans knew that he had screwed up. He also knew he may have damaged his aircraft, so he reported the incident. Squadron mechanics thoroughly reviewed the plane's structural integrity, including rivets, that were repaired or replaced. He never again executed a loop in afterburner.

The average person does not realize how many military people are killed in training accidents. In World War II the Germans lost 20 percent of their fliers due to avoidable accidents. The great Luftwaffe ace Hans-

Joachim Marseille, who shot down 154 mostly British aircraft and 13 in one day died in a dubious accident. Preventable accidents killed German aces Nowotny (258 kills) and Bar (220 kills).

The SAC Brat learns to fly. Well, sort of. One day my father took me flying from Offutt Air Force Base in a small aircraft, likely a Piper Cub. Colonel Evans gave Don Evans, the SAC Brat, the controls. It scared the daylights out of me as the plane wobbled around. I would like to tell the reader I proceeded to do a few loops and roll overs, but the truth is that I quickly asked my father to take the controls. While I have never been nervous about flying under another pilot's control, for example a commercial or private pilot, I have never had the interest in becoming a pilot.

I recall seeing one of the revolutionary Lockheed F-104s Starfighters on the field. The Starfighter featured a radical design, with thin, stubby wings attached further back on the fuselage than most contemporary aircraft. The wing provided excellent supersonic and high-speed-low - altitude performance, but also poor turning capability and high landing speeds. It was the first aircraft to achieve Mach 2, and the first aircraft to reach an altitude of 100,000 feet after taking off under its own power. Starfighter established world records in speed, altitude, and time-to-climb in 1958, becoming the first aircraft to hold all three simultaneously. I learned years later that the airplane had been sold by the United States to NATO countries. The Germans lost 292 of 916 aircraft and 116 pilots from 1961 to 1989, leading the German public to dub the Starfighter the "widow maker". The F-104 upgrade fighter training was very dangerous.

After three years at SAC Headquarters, my father packed up our family and headed south to Fort Worth, Texas. I do not recall it as a big deal. I don't recall how I felt about missing some of my Bellevue friends. I guess I assumed I would see them at another base and I looked forward to the new base, new friends and new adventure in Texas. Perhaps due to the periodic moves SAC Brats and military Brats in general just accept that is just part of the way life is. The best way to describe a move for a boy my age is like a dog. The dog doesn't mind changes in location as long as it's with its owner. My anchor was not the location but my parents and sister.

I always enjoyed the Robert Duval movie, *The Great Santini.* There is a scene in which the Marine Corps family is moving to a new location alone in their car at night. It is the family isolated against the world so to speak. My family felt like that in our move from Nebraska to Carswell Air Force Base in Fort Worth, Texas. We sang songs and played games in the car just like the fictional family in the movie. The difference was that my father was a light-drinker and certainly not the border line almost insane, brutish character of Duval in the movie.

I gained considerable insight reading Kris Kristofferson's book about being a military Brat. Kristofferson's father was not in SAC but was an Air Force general. Kris indicated that his sister had a far more difficult time than guys with parents in the military. Likely periodic moves appeared to disturb girls, who tend to be more socially-oriented with their girlfriends and surroundings. They would establish stronger social interactions which inflicted deep emotional stress when separating a few years later. I think this was true of my sister Barbara, who was not thrilled by our move to Texas. At the same time the Brats had a feeling of pride in what their fathers were doing for their country and in a way, we thought we were making a small contribution ourselves.

I shared the Kristofferson book with the wife of a good friend. She was an Army Brat so I thought she would enjoy the book. She was retired but previously had been third in rank in a large metropolitan police department. My buddy told me that after reading the book, she cried. The girls likely made greater sacrifices than the boys by absorbing the changes in friends and locations that were required. It was an adventure for the boys.

My Mom was pleased in that it located us closer to her parents in San Antonio. My mom also had some friends in Fort Worth and had fun in college visiting the River Crest Country Club there in Fort Worth.

General Jack Catton, one of the youngest officers to make general in the U. S. military was my father's boss at Offutt. In his annual review of my father's performance General Catton stated that my father was almost a "servant to his honesty." Richard Evans might have been described as a Don Quixote type of man. He was very idealistic in his love of country and the Air Force mission. While he faced death, he loved life and was anything but a brutish person. In the highly acclaimed movie, *The Right Stuff* the strait-laced John Glenn character evoked memories of my Old Man's character. I know that today the Air Force still possesses the same type of men.

General Jack Catton endured polio (poliomyelitis), the highly contagious disease caused by the polio virus, which attacks the nervous system causing irreversible paralysis. Through personal strength and perseverance, he not only would have to battle polio, but he recovered. He then advanced to be the three star Commander of the 15th Air Force of SAC at March Field and the eventual the four-star Commander of the Military Air Command.

Richard Evans and his family were off to Texas. Richard, being the son of a dedicated high school teacher and principal, wanted to take advantage of the available time gained from being in the car during extended driving legs. With captive time to teach his Brats my dad would give us SAC math problems. Here is an example. You are flying in a B-52 at 550 miles an hour with a headwind of 50 miles an hour. You must travel 1000 miles. It is 1200 hours, what time is your ETA? My sister Barbara and I loved this little challenge as we competed to answer the problem.

Fort Worth had 250,000 inhabitants mainly centered on the aerospace industry along with farming, cattle and oil. The people in the town were patriots. Not far from Carswell AFB was a highway made of red bricks leading out of the western part of town called Camp Bowie. The highway, named after a World War I Army training camp, used to prepare Doughboys for combat in Europe. The use of the name was appropriate since Jim Bowie was one of the heroes of the Alamo. There was a street named Foch to honor the French Allied Commander during that war. A giant Convair aircraft manufacturing complex stretched across the western side of the Carswell Air Force Base runway. On the north side of the Convair plant was Lake Worth, a SAC Brat's paradise.

Fort Worth, like all cities, had a group of "City Fathers" mostly to advocate for the benefit of the town. I am perhaps biased but for its size Fort Worth punched above its weight. It had a world class art museum, a world-famous concert piano player named Van Cliburn who beat the

Russians at their own game in Moscow, soon a Speaker of the United States House of Representatives, Texas Christian University, the Will Roger's Coliseum, the highly regarded Fort Worth Rodeo, some very rich oil men, and a founder of American Airlines. Also included were two nationally ranked, first-class golf courses, River Crest and Colonial, the latter being the home of Ben Hogan.

When the Evans crew showed up at Carswell in 1957, we moved into a four-bedroom officer's home. There were two officers attached residences in which they knocked down the middle walls to create a larger place. Beauty was not the issue, space was. My sister lived on the far side of the house across from my parents. On one side there was a dining room while its duplicate was made into a living room. I was on the other side of the house and the duplicate to my room was our TV room. The entrée to the house had a room on each side, one of which hosted a ping pong table. The house was very functional.

Our house was located a quarter mile from the fence separating the runway from the rest of the base. When my father's B-58s taxied to a stop, the screeching sound hurt your ears. It was startling. The Officer's Club with pool was a quarter of a mile north next to attractive Lake Worth. The Trinty River ran next to the base on its east side. There was a playground at back of the house, plenty of trees to climb or to build a fort, room to shoot BB guns and an added advantage for a SAC Brat a red ant hill with large ants we could blow up with firecrackers or M-80s. This place was SAC Brat Heaven.

We later learned the airmen's club was nearby with a huge pool. Burger's Lake, with high swings and diving platforms, was down the Trinity River. What a deal.

Joe Yahr was my best friend, who lived a few houses down the street. Our summer activities focused on enjoying Lake Worth. It was on Lake Worth that Colonel Trimble and Burt taught me to water ski. Burt lived off base.

Joe and I would take a twenty-foot seine to catch huge crayfish and brim in the shallows. We'd take my kayak out on the lake and watch the B-58s screaming over our heads. We'd go to the Officers' Club pool and dive. Sometimes we would get up early with other buddies and sneak under the base's east perimeter fence to get down to the Trinity River. There was plenty of undergrowth so you could barely see the river from the base. We'd catch fish and sometimes fry cut-up hot dogs for breakfast. We could get into Burger's Lake from the Trinity River or "free" side which allowed us to have fun being more independent.

I recall thinking several times as I exited and entered Carswell AFB's fence line to explore the Trinity River, that security seemed nonexistent near those fences and thick trees. The Brats did not climb over the fences- we went under them. In my childhood I thought that if I could sneak in, couldn't a saboteur? Perhaps we were being watched but I never saw any Air Police in the area. Today Carswell is no longer a SAC base but the several hundred yard fence line along the Trinity River has been cleared of trees likely to allow security a clear view of that area off the base.

Several of the Brats grabbed their sleeping bags to camp out behind my house. It was a hundred treeless yards to the main road and an intersection on the corner. Since it was late there were few cars going by. Someone made a dare that we should run naked to the light and back. Three or four of us took off buck naked for the light. As we approached the intersection a SAC patrol truck came into view and so did we. We all stopped and then turned tail and ran back to get our clothes on. The air policemen in the truck, sensing that we did not appear dangerous, just ignored us.

I learned a lot about the Bible at the base Sunday School. Our parents would sleep in on Sunday and Barbara and I were required to get dressed and walk a quarter mile to the school. After Sunday School, our parents would often take us to the Officer's Club for Sunday dinner. I think that both our mom and dad had a lot of church experience during the Depression and World War II. At the end of the day on a base either *Retreat* or the *Star Spangled Banner* were played as the flag was lowered on base. People would stop what they were doing and get out of cars and stand at attention or salute in respect.

Colonel Richard Evans and his B-58 test crew

Barbara and Don Evans departing for Sunday School at Carswell Air Force Base

My friends and I enrolled in Burton Hill Elementary School which was off base. My sister Barbara went to Stripling Middle School. A bus would pick us up and take us to the school. The kids were a mix of SAC Brats and working-class Texas kids.

Not long after our Carswell arrival, the Evans family was invited to dinner with the Deutschendorf. Major Henry Deutschendorf had been recruited by my father to join the B-58 Test program. My father and his colleagues had great respect for the flying abilities of Major "Dutch" Deutschendorf. The major, like my father, had extensive experience in midair refueling. My sister, who is four years older than me, remembers several times that we visited the family. During our visits Barbara joined Major Deutschendorf's son John in his room listening to him play the guitar.

It was Major Deutschendorf who set several world speed records in the B-58. His son John and my sister Barbara attended Arlington Heights High School. John changed his last name to John Denver. John became one of the most popular music artists of the 1970s. I was not aware that John Dutchenford and John Denver were the same guy until years later. While I was attending the University of Southern California, my father told me that his old friend Henry was in Los Angeles and called to catch up. In the conversation Henry told my father he was not flying for the Air Force any longer but for his son as his pilot.

Denver became an accomplished pilot, most likely due to his father's influence, and was type-rated to fly his personal Lear Jet. John lost his life flying a new model aircraft in which the fuel system control switch design was faulty. While airborne, he was unable to prevent aircraft fuel starvation by switching fuel tanks. Ironically multiple B-58 accidents were the result of imbalanced fuel loads jeopardizing the stability of the aircraft.

I bet that if Johnny Deutschendorf were alive today, he would indicate that his proudest days were as a SAC Brat and not as an entertainer. I bet that he, like myself, considered our fathers better men for their sacrifice on behalf of our country. John Denver's first big hit was the song which he wrote and made popular by the group Peter Paul and Mary, *I'm Leaving on a Jet Plane.*

It is interesting that two great musical artists grew up in military families, Kris Kristofferson and John Denver. Add to those gentlemen Jim

Morrison of the Doors. His father was a Navy admiral equivalent to an Air Force General.

While I was having adventures at Burton Hill with Joe Yahr, my father almost got killed again. He was landing a B-58, which required an unusually steep angle. The nose had to rotate up so that the tires near the back of the aircraft would catch the load at touchdown. The pilot's forward visibility was seriously impeded when the nose was way up in a landing. My father came in with the nose too high, inducing his two back engines to impact the runway. He immediately called a briefing of his multiple test crews to explain his error and to ensure others learned from his mistake. The challenge of flying the B-58 was that the cutting-edge, fragile aerodynamic design permitted no aircrew deviation from the tight mission profile. The Hustler was far ahead of its time but only the most highly proficient pilot could survive. B-58 pilots were the best of the best.

My father told me about a game he played with his buddy who was Wing Commander of B-52s back in 1958. I do not recall the officer's name. When there was a guest at Barksdale Air Force Base that knew my father, his buddy would suggest they all have lunch at the officer's club. The guest would be told that Colonel Evans is on the other side of the base and would meet them. My father would get a call at Carswell 500 miles or more away. He'd hop into an F-102 and meet the officers for lunch.

Colonel Richard Evans, as the Commanding Officer of the brand-new Mach 2 B-58 bomber test program that had just been established in Fort Worth and Jo Ann Evans, my bueatiful mother, became acquainted with an influential core of Fort Worth civic and industry leaders. Fort Worth clearly understood the fiscal value and national security pride of hosting the pioneering state-of-the-art program. In addition to trusted friendships that developed, several members of both groups enjoyed water skiing. The Evans soon found themselves invited to the luxurious River Crest Country Club for dinners and parties. Our family also traveled to the Eagle Mountain Boat Club north of Fort Worth to ski and party. It was an exclusive club where a Texas oil man had his big yacht anchored on a freshwater lake. Only in Texas! I never saw a bald eagle or a mountain near that lake. But again, that is Texas!

I met Gary Laughlin an oil developer, Hunter Barret, a real estate developer, Tom Law, a highly respected attorney and civic leader, Elton Hyder, an attorney that served at the Tojo Trials in Japan and Amon Carter Jr. whose father helped establish American Airlines and owned the Fort Worth local newspaper. It was exceptional for me as a young person to be exposed to and learn about these people, listen to their views and accomplishments. Older people do not realize how much younger people benefit by just listening to the chit chat that goes on. It was a reset of my experience having access to Strategic Air Command executives, but in a very different setting.

I cannot emphasize enough how important the messages adults communicate are when children are present. Children should pay close attention to what successful older adults say or advise. Adults have valuable experience which is history to the kids. In the animal world adults communicate lessons to the pups and if those offspring listen, they will avoid many mistakes and benefit from the wisdom of parental experience. Too often in our society young people are being influenced by the media which I assume includes the internet. Unlike parents that have a natural love and hope for their youngsters' success, the internet advice is to promote spending and profit for the internet and media owners. This not only provides terribly biased advice but enslavement via increasing personal debt. The government often provides the same poor messaging and thus disservice.

One answer for children lacking a father figure or parents to pass on valuable information to achieve a free and successful life is mentoring. Successful adults that "give back" in their later years via mentoring a young person do a service for that child and our nation. Those people that mentor young people also derive great benefit in the process.

After retiring I had the pleasure of being a mentor in a program called Quest for Kids. The child was an eight-grade Haitian American. Eight years later he had graduated from NC State and was starting his own business. I cannot claim any credit for his success, but I do think I was a positive influence and I learned a lot. I know he worked hard and that the Quest for Kids program was well thought out.

This is an area in which those that argue about white privilege have a point. If people, regardless of race, are the best trained group and run the upper echelons of a nation, the children that can grow up embedded in that information flow enjoy a greater advantage. It is not solely an issue of race. Its positional or class level. As a SAC Brat with my parents interacting with powerful and successful Air Force and civilians' personnel, I enjoyed great advantage over a kid of any race or heritage whose father painted houses and whose conversations with his friends were about whether the Yankees would win the pennant.

This SAC Brat benefited greatly due to the mentoring of many people. My father was naturally the leader in this process for me. I gained great insight thanks to the mentoring of my stepfather, a civilian, Tom Law. During key times in my development, my grandfather, Jean Nelson, provided leadership for me as well as my father's brother, Tom Evans. None of these men are with us today, but they live on.

Colonel Richard Evans was required to divert from his Carswell duties to comply with an order to sit on a promotion board in Washington D.C. The distinguished officers selected as members reviews were decision making bodies determining whether an officer's record would qualify him, when compared with his peers, to move up the promotion ladder. My father was chosen as a judge in this role.

"You picked a fine time to leave me Lucille" by Kenny Rogers describes what happened next.

While in D.C. and at the Pentagon, Colonel Evans dropped into the office of his ultimate boss, Four-Star General Curtis LeMay. They had been respected friends from the Tinian Days during World War II in the Pacific, MacDill AFB, Florida flying B-47's, including setting the 35-hour refueling record and Offutt's SAC headquarters as a member of LeMay's staff. The Chief of Staff of the United States Air Force asked the officer he deeply respected, Colonel Evans, a straightforward question. What was his personal and professional operational judgement of the B-58? General LeMay was assured that he would receive a direct, unvarnished judgement from his trusted B-58 chief test pilot. He was correct. My father stated that the aircraft was a limited range, delectate, operational challenge, even for an above average pilot and that the B-58 might be more mission effective if assigned to the Tactical Air Command (TAC). Examples of short-range tactical aircraft would have been the F4 Phantom, F-105 Thunderbird and the RF-101C Voodoo photoreconnaissance aircraft. Both men were aware of the development of the longer range and much faster B-70 which could come online in 7-8 years.

Colonel Evans returned to Carswell Air Force Base. Within a few days, he was told by his immediate boss General John McConnell that a new officer would be assuming command over the B-58 Test Program. Richard Evans was likely going to be the new Base Commander at Carswell, which to Richard Evans would be like being a janitor in a high school in which you were the principal. My father was told by General McConnell, "you will never make General Officer." I assume McConnell was extremely unhappy with my father's view and that in McConnell's eyes Colonel Evans had gone above the chain of command. It is also feasible that the General was a sponsor of the B-58 program within the Air Force.

In his later years, my father told me that he noticed that he was being followed at Carswell by some non-uniformed men. He later told me they were called Special Services. My father did suffer from Alzheimers in his last 15 years of life, but I heard about the Special Services 25 years prior to his death and years before he wrote his book. I have no idea if these people existed or what they did for SAC.

My father was alarmed enough to visit a General Officer and buddy who was at Eglin Field in Florida to get his advice. He was told it would blow over.

In General, McConnell's annual review of Colonel Richard Evans, there was no praise or criticism of Colonel Evans' performance. There was a reference to the fact that Colonel Evans was getting along well with the local community. McConnell was surprised that my father made the difficult decision to leave the Air Force. This was unusual because Richard Evans only had 3 years left in the service and when completed he would have received 50 percent of active-duty Colonel's pay every month for the rest of his life.

The B-58 was never deployed in combat. Tragically, 111 were built and 26 crashed, an astonishing accident rate of 24.5 percent.

Chapter 16: Los Angeles and the B-70 Project

Twenty years later I was on active duty in United States Air Force in the Military Airlift Command stationed at Norton AFB. I was one of three other college graduates who were lowly airmen in the Air Lift Command Element (ALCE). Our function was to do odd jobs for the officers. We were called "go fors" which meant we were ordered to "go for this or go for that." In a conversation with one of the navigators, he mentioned that he had been stationed at Carswell AFB in the late 1950s. I asked if he had been a member of the B-58 Test program and he answered in the affirmative. I told him that my father was Colonel Richard Evans. He then gave me a comment that I am very proud of. He said, "Your father Colonel Richard Evans was the best Air Force officer I ever knew." The navigator then looked at me and must have thought "the apple can fall far from the tree."

I asked my father years later if he should have initiated his meeting with LeMay at the Pentagon. As head of the B-58 Test Program and having established a decade long bridge of faith with the AF Chief of Staff, Richard Evans should have anticipated LeMay's question. The B-58 was designed to be the heir to the B-52 in the future all-important deterrence mission for SAC. In initiating a private meeting with the trusted Chief of Staff, the potential risk was responding too honestly to questions that should have been directed at my father's boss, General McConnell. When he learned of the meeting McConnell clearly took offense. He must have concluded that his junior officer was going over his head. I do not think that my father meant disrespect to his superior. He visited an old friend and believed his response would be unofficial if asked. This same idealism or even naivety motivated my father to leave the Air Force when he could have stayed on in Fort Worth for three years and collected his Colonel's retirement benefits. As stated, General McConnel in his report showed great surprise that any officer would forgo early retirement benefits and leave the Air Force early. General McConnell was later a four-star general and Chief of Staff of the Air Force.

My father left SAC and the Air Force because he concluded that his follow-on assignment would be tangential to the preeminent mission of being combat ready to defend our nation. North American Aviation won the contract to build the next generation XB-70 Valkyrie, the Mach 3 plus, six engine, delta wing, long range bomber that my father had conceptualized for General LeMay during his headquarters SAC assignment. In recognition of his expertise, the North American leadership hired him to share his strategic vision of effective deterrence and his strategic bomber operation mastery as a highly credible source to better inform the leadership of the Executive and Congressional branches of government. Richard Evans was an unmatched ambassador on behalf of the B-70 Valkyrie. Colonel Evans also informed dignitaries at North American on the Appollo and Saturn rocket programs.

The Evans family and the SAC Brats were moving again and back to Los Angeles. If my father was no longer in SAC but he was working with SAC to develop the most controversial weapon up to that time in SAC history. Did I still qualify for this elite group of kids? I thought so.

The stress of life in meeting the unrelenting ultimatums of the Strategic Air Command mission finally took its toll on our family. My mother did not want to leave Fort Worth and move again. She was sick of the unpredictable, periodic uprooting and moving. The net result of my father's relocation to accept his new civilian job in Los Angeles was the "straw that broke the camel's back" of my parents' marriage. My parents planned a divorce.

After my mother investigated a home to rent near Burton Hill Elementary, she changed her mind. Then we were off to Los Angeles. We settled in a lovely executive style home in the Pacific Palisades, an affluent neighborhood tucked away between the Sana Monica Mountains and the Pacific Ocean. My sister Barbara entered Paul Revere High School, as I enrolled in the sixth grade at Palisades Elementary. I liked the school and enjoyed going to the beach during the weekends. My father became immersed addressing his responsibility working and representing North American Aviation concentrating on the Mach 3 B-70 program.

With the Soviets and the United States in a self-destructive missile competition it was only a matter of time in which one side would find the solution to launching a high-speed missile capable of shooting down an ultra-high-altitude, high-speed airplane. The ongoing counter argument presented by the United States defense companies advocating long range missiles was the superior choice relative to bombers was countered by bomber advocates. The bomber advocates' strongest argument was that with a human in the cockpit a bomber could be launched but could be recalled back at the last minute. Missiles, in contrast, once fired could not be aborted. There was a finality about missiles while manned bombers offered maximum human flexibility.

While in the Palisades, I experienced behavior by a civilian kid growing up in our upscale neighborhood that gave me the idea of what many civilians thought was important. The boy implied that it was demeaning that my family was renting a home. He said something like, "you live in a rented home" clearly coaching his phrase as an insult. My reaction was one of being surprised and confused that this fellow would think he could humiliate me. If he said, "your father is a coward," or "your mother is ugly," I would have been annoyed, but "you rent a house?" My feelings were not hurt for I had almost always lived in a government supported or rented home along with my Brat friends.

I quickly concluded that he and any cohorts playing lip service to the flag and pretending to be patriots, were protected, isolated young men, without a clue regarding military dedication and sacrifice, are lost on their own narrow egos. Their distorted value system is driven by acquiring material objects and external shallow entitlements, dramatically opposed the commitment of service families on behalf of national defense over self, protecting the security and freedom of our fellow citizens day and night. Many civilians with this point of view undoubtedly feel guilt, thus viewing military members and their families as suckers or abnormal people that want to fight. The sad point is that if too many civilians think that way we will lose our country.

Too many civilians do not want to defend and fight for something bigger than themselves, specifically their country. We would be a better and stronger nation if all our children after graduation served two years in the service of our country, as all males were required to do prior to the end of the mandatory military draft in 1973 which market the transition to an all-volunteer force. High school graduates were ordered to report to the United States Army for a two-year enlistment within 90 days. Within the 90-day interim period, draftees were offered the option of enlisting in the Navy or Marine Corps for three years or the Air Force for four years. An exception was allowed for students choosing to pursue college education. Members of the latter category were required to carry a minimum of 15 hours every semester or quarter and were sworn in as cadets of the Army, Navy, or Air Force ROTC units, thus earning commissions upon graduation. Individuals failing to meet the standard were immediately drafted into the Army. It is estimated that approximately 24 countries require mandatory military service. In most cases that very process instills in the individual involved a greater appreciation for one's country.

After six months in California, my mother packed us up and drove Barbara and me back to Fort Worth. I should have refused to leave but I thought my primary responsibility was to protect my mother. Richard Evans returned home from Washington, after lobbying members of Congress to support funding the B-70, to find an empty house.

I re-enrolled in Burton Hill in the winter of 1959. Monning Junior High followed in 1960. On May 1, 1960, a plane was shot down by a Soviet surface-to-air missile while flying through Soviet airspace at high altitude of 70,000 feet. The victims were the high-altitude U-2 spy plane and the CIA pilot Francis Gary Powers.

Powers ejected and parachuted safely to the ground, where he was captured by the KGB, and held for interrogation. The plane crashed, but parts of it were recovered and placed on public display in Moscow evidence of "American deceit." The fallout over the incident resulted in a cancellation of the Paris Summit scheduled to discuss the ongoing situation in divided Germany, the possibility of an arms control or test ban treaty, and the relaxation tensions between the USSR and the United States.

History can be so strange. After 21 months in a Russian prison, Powers was freed and returned to the United States. After years of flying dangerous U-2 missions he got a "safe" job flying a TV news helicopter over Los Angeles. Unbelievably, in 1977 after reporting on a brush fire, his helicopter ran out of fuel. Powers died crashing into a Los Angeles public school athletic field. No one on the ground was injured.

The manned bombers' days appeared to be limited if facing a Russian missile capable of shooting down an airplane flying at a 70,000-foot-high altitude. It would be a matter of time before surface-to-air missiles (SAMS) would attain the speed to catch and destroy our bomber force at high altitudes. The B-58 and B-70 programs were threatened. They depended on high speed and altitude to strike and safely exit the target. High Mach missiles were shredding those advantages.

There were three evolving answers aside from the United States building a fleet of ICBMs. First, the United State could build aircraft with terrain-following radar (TFR) to avoid radar detection. Second, adapt high-speed, long-range missiles fired from stand-off B-52s. The B-52 aircraft could cover the necessary distance to reach the required position to launch missiles that possess sufficient range and speed to penetrate and strike the target. The last option was stealth technology. That is, design a manned aircraft that emitted an undetectable radar signal allowing unrestricted overflight access. Examples of successful stealth technology include the Northrop B-2 Spirit stealth bomber and the Northrop RQ-180 highly classified American stealth unmanned aerial vehicle (UAV) designed for high-altitude, long endurance (HALE) intelligence, surveillance, and reconnaissance (ISR) in highly contested airspace.

Don Evans, always a SAC Brat, was faced with the dilemma of attempting to figure out life and his place therein as the result of his father and mother's divorce. My mother married Tom Law and continued to reside in Fort Worth. It was the same year that dozens of African nations declared their independence from their colonial mother countries. They concluded that removing their white overlords would open the door to prosperity. In America the Civil Rights movement was heating up. Many black people believed that better education driven by equal rights would resolve the extremes of wealth in America.

With the election of President Jack Kennedy, my country continued to be frozen in a Cold War against the communist bloc of the Soviet

Union, China, North Vietnam, Cuba and North Korea. The North Vietnamese were gradually invading South Vietnam, and the United States opted to intervene.

Being a SAC Brat, I took the story of the French and English sellout of Czechoslovakia to the Nazis at Munich in 1938 as gospel. I did not understand why a nation would appease another's demands. I had been taught that the only way to avoid war was through strength. Strength and deterrence defined the Strategic Air Command. I experienced this lesson at a personal level growing up. It seemed that each time I moved to a new school, one of the boys would start a fight with me. If I had been much larger, the SAC lesson would apply, and no one would have dared. Unfortunately for me, my opponents were always some boy a grade or two higher. My brief fight record was to win two out of three encounters. Once these minor incidences ended, my opponent and I were almost friends. There was a school yard respect because I would not be bullied. There was a balance of power. I would not be tested again at that school. I think a lot of young men go through this particularly if they are new in a school.

The Paul Neuman movie *Cool Hand Luke* tells a terrific story in which a weaker man has no chance against a far more powerful adversary in a fight. The difference is the willingness of the weaker man to refuse defeat and thus wins the admiration of the others. He achieves victory in defeat and becomes the leader of the group. Is a mouse standing up to a cat braver than a bear? In the jungle of world competition, are some nations so pugnacious that they are free from larger, more powerful ones? Have some nations stayed free because the larger powers view them as not worth the price needed to subjugate them? This would seem true of the Picts and Germans verses Rome in 150 AD and the Finns, Swiss, Afghans and North Koreans in our time.

The Strategic Air Command was all about deterrence. I completely accepted the idea of a monolithic communist block determined to destroy the West. My mother and I used to have spirited debates about whether the Vietnam War was a monolithic communist push, or as she viewed the subject, a Vietnamese revolution in which the people were fighting to not be colonies or pawns of the major powers but independent nations.

My mother was right and I was wrong. The Vietnamese leaders were communists, but they were fighting to reverse the European empire's conquest of the Third World. This struggle was going on all over the world as the colonies of the prior century were coming of age. The most powerful issue was nationalism.

The old colonial powers in the form of the Soviet Union, the United States and nations of Europe were still fighting among themselves for control or influence in these new nations. The result was an acceleration of European decline in the World. As in World War I and World War II, the Third World or former colonies were attempting to play the white Europeans against one another for their advantage.

Leon Trotski, leader of the Soviet Red Army under Lenin, challenged Stalin over the issue of priority of internationalism or nationalism in the 20s and 30s. Trotsky lost and Stalin had him assassinated. Stalin's focus on nationalism prevailed. President Woodrow Wilson and Ambassador Henry Cabot Lodge engaged in a bloodless debate on the same subject. Lodge carried the day, preventing the United States from entering the League of Nations.

The Vietnamese were delighted to secure Russian and Chinese aid against the Americans. Once the United States was driven out of Southeast Asia the Vietnamese nationalists became concerned with the Chinese and Cambodians as potential threats. The Vietnamese national history had suffered periods of war with China and Cambodia. Within a few years the Vietnamese invaded neighboring Cambodia. Conversely, they had to fight off a Chinese invasion of Vietnam. Clearly, communism was not a monolithic force immune to nationalism.

The Russians, influenced by nationalism, initiated a border war with their former Chinese communist ally. The Chinese, retaining a memory of the Russian Czars taking vast amounts of Chinese lands in the 19th century's "Unequal Treaties", readily engaged the Russians.

With the United States no longer the threat, the Chinese and Russians approached their former capitalists adversaries as long-lost friends, as they attempted to recruit the United States to help their competing nationalistic causes.

Stalin, Lodge and Jo Ann Law, my mother were right. Communism was not a monolithic force uniting all communists. Nationalism, with its shared culture, people and language, was the ultimate force driving the nations of the world.

One of my father's books, written by a Frenchman Michel Garder got my attention while I was a senior in high school. It was entitled "L'Agone du Regina en Russie Sovietique" or *The Death Struggle of the Regime in Soviet Russia.* Garder predicted that the Soviet Union, like all the European empires in the late 20th century, would collapse. One of the main themes was the low Russian birthrate compared to the high Muslim birthrate within the Soviet Union. The author predicted that the Muslims would eventually outnumber the Russian population. Second, he pointed out the many divisions in language and religion in the Soviet empire. While the Russian empire was connected by land and the European mainly via navies and water, both systems suffered due to the differences in the people. The author predicted the forces facing the Soviet Union were parallel to those bringing down the European systems. The Soviets looked far too strong to me at the time, but Michel Garder was correct.

While the United States had a more homogeneous population and was almost self-sufficient, it could be argued then and now that the United States could suffer the same fate as the Soviet Union. Henry Kissinger seemed to realize this long-term likelihood when he wrote *A World Restored: Metternich, Castlereagh and the Problems of Peace 1812-1822.* Prince Metternich guided the policy of the divided Austro-Hungarian Empire and likely extended its life via his diplomatic skill. Capitalistic President Richard Nixon, invoking his geopolitical strategy of paring communist Russian nationalism off against communist Chinese nationalism, likely extended the power of the United States. No, it was not about ping pong.

The quandary long term was the result of President Lyndon Johnson's policies. Johnson opened immigration to millions of people that had little in common with the predominantly European United States. Disciplines were eliminated concerning the "Americanization" of newcomers. Citizens were not required to vote in English. The sinews that held the nation in common were balkanized. The country gradually became more divided.

America's success made its people lazy and dependent on the government verses their predecessors who contributed to their host government. I am convinced this is a natural process as a successful nation matures. In the late 20th century, the freed colonial powers were gaining on the former mother countries via higher populations and a willingness to do the dirty jobs associated with industrialization. From 1950 to 2026 United States manufacturing fell from 50 percent to 12 percent of world production. American economist defined the United States as a "mature economy" with a massive service industry. America decreased reliance on productive power, deferring to foreign nations as the source. Perhaps I am wrong, but equating the GDP generated by the beauty business in the United States of $308 billion to China's $351 billion spent on defense are not equal in measuring national strength.

In the early 1960s, the United States and Russian persistently continued their space and arms race with the focus on ICBMs. Production of the B-58 terminated at 111 aircraft. Exactly two B-70s were built. Convair aerospace company became General Dynamics and began to produce the F-111, the Aardvark, for the SAC arsenal. The Aardvark was equipped with Advanced Terran Following Radar which could fly below the radar beams with ground hugging equipment.

In November 1963, my stepfather Tom Law invited me to join him at a breakfast meeting with the guest of honor President Jack Kennedy. Being a foolish teenager and not a great fan of President Kennedy, my first response was to ask how early I would have to get up to attend. Tom indicated around 6:00 A.M. Tom rightfully concluded I was not the man for the job. A few days later I asked him about breakfast, and he explained that due to my delay in deciding he had invited a business associate. I had missed the boat. This, of course, was the breakfast Kennedy attended in Fort Worth prior to his assassination.

I regret my delay which resulted in my missing this historic event. Another part of me is glad for I cannot imagine the effect or feelings I would have had seeing the President and perhaps having the chance to shake his hand and then knowing he was murdered hours later.

Tommy Schiefer, brother of CBS newsman Bob Schieffer, was a classmate. I was standing in the lunch line at Arlington Heights High

School with buddy Whit Smith when Tommy came up to us and said, "Kennedy has been assassinated". I told Tommy, "No way, I will bet $5 it isn't true". My closest friend from Junior High, John Hawkins, later supplied further evidence. John's older brother Dr. Thomas Hawkins was an intern at Parkland Hospital in Dallas when the President was brought in. According to Thomas, it was hard to reconcile that Kennedy was struck from the front when his exit wounds appeared in the back of his head. We later learned that Oswald had briefly been a student in our school the same year as Thomas Hawkins. Oswald was even in the *Yellow Jacket yearbook* with his picture taken in the lab which was my homeroom.

I continued to live in Fort Worth, visiting my father in California during the summer, until my junior year in high school. My SAC Brat buddy Joe Yahr and his family had been transferred. Jack Ridley, whose father was killed in a military aircraft accident, lived down the street. I fondly remember his widowed mother. Our SAC friends, the Jansens retired in Fort Worth. Colonel Jansen's oldest son Carl went to the Air Force Academy and played football. I relocated to join my father in Palos Verdes, California in 1964.

As the B-70 program wound down, my father continued to work for North American in a marketing capacity. His responsibilities broadened from the B-70 to work on the X-15, Saturn and Apollo Spacecraft programs. North American Aviation was the primary contractor for the massive Saturn rocket. This rocket produced at the Rocketdyne Division generated so much thrust that it was 50 years before America built engines more powerful. Paul Castenholz was the American born Vice President for the division. Paul Castenholz was the project manager for the Redstone, Jupiter, Thor and Saturn rocket engines. The Saturn engine enabled the United States to go to the moon. I remember Paul and how much my father respected the man. I recall conversations concerning how engine efficiency was so dependent on the high-speed pumps.

The North American X-15 was an Air Force hypersonic rocket-powered experimental aircraft. The X-15 set speed and altitude records in the 1960s, crossing the edge of outer space and returning with valuable data. The X-15's highest speed, 4,520 miles pe hour flying Mach 6.7 at an altitude of 340,100 feet or 67miles. The rocket powered jet set the official world record for the highest speed ever recorded by a crew powered aircraft and remains unbroken.

A friend of my father at North American Aviation was a pilot and engineer named Scott Crossfield. Chuck Yeager is famous for being the first man to fly faster than the speed of sound Mach One. Depending on altitude and temperature, this is approximately 710 miles per hour. Crossfield was the first man to fly twice the speed of sound. Both pilots are shown favorably in the movie *The Right Stuff*.

Scott Crossfield was the most recognized test pilot of the X-15 program. Crossfield would be strapped into the seat of his X-15 with the aircraft attached to a B-52. The B-52 would fly to 50,0000 feet and then release the X-15. Scott Crossfield would ignite the X-15 rocket engines, and the aircraft would travel to the edge of space. Scott would then glide the aircraft back to the Edwards Air Force Base dry lake field. This experiment was done repeatedly to learn how to return spacecraft to earth. It is the basis of the Space Shuttle re-entry. In his professional life, my father did not spend his time and effort involved in minor league programs or with those who lacked vision.

Scott Crossfield was the fastest man on earth in a single seat airplane. I recall in 1963 when I lived with my mother, stepdad, baby brother, baby sister and sister in Texas, receiving a signed photo from Scott Crossfield in front of the X-15. It was one of the perks for a SAC Brat during those days. This great American hero and pioneer was to retire from North American only to be killed in a small Cessna private aircraft. Scott Crossfield was flying from Alabama at night to his home near Manassa, Virginia and was caught in a thunderstorm. The aircraft wreckage indicated his plane was ripped apart by the storm prior to crashing. This American hero that risked his life countless times flying with dangerous new technology was to die in a private aircraft. Sometimes, truth is stranger than fiction.

Scott Crossfield and X-15

B-70 on the factory floor

Colonel Richard Evans and General Jimmy Stewart admiring a B-70 model

After the 1969 moon landings, the aerospace industry went into a recession. The Rockwell Company acquired North American Aviation. This great company pioneered by Dutch Kindelberger and Lee Atwood was now a division of Rockwell. The great company built the P-51, arguably the best propeller driven fighter of World War II. It built the F-86 Saber, sometimes known as the Saber Jet that established a claimed kill ratio of over 10 to 1 of Migs in the Korean War. It built the F-100 Super Saber, America's first supersonic fighter. If there was a company that represented the guts of our ability to go to the moon, it was North American Aviation, Inc. They built the Saturn rocket booster and the Apollo Spacecraft.

As the aerospace industry and North American Aviation spun down, Richard Evans found himself out of a full-time job. Although he enjoyed a distinguished Air Force and exceptional civilian aerospace career, he no longer retained the security of regular full-time employment, nor had he established Air Force retirement income. Often in adversity in life, strong people overcompensate. My father turned to consulting working for Northrop Corporation and Douglas Aircraft. He earned more money working as a consultant than on his salaried income. This served as a great lesson for me as I realized that in a capitalistic country, at the executive or higher level, there is a positive correlation between enhanced income and job risk. At mid-level this is not true since the average government employee makes 35 percent greater net pay verses his civilian counterpart. Richard Evans was out of a job. The result for my father was consulting work for Northrup Corporation and Douglas Aircraft.

While at North American Aviation, my father became an expert at creating military briefings using double slides to communicate the aerospace engineer's ideas to a military or civilian leader. I recall his work with the Douglas Aircraft Company when they competed for the C-5A and the fact that the aircraft was designed around its ability to carry two Abrams tanks. Douglas lost the competition to Lockheed.

The Northrop Corporation's competition for the Stealth B-2 Spirit proved more successful. The Germans in World War II arguably built a stealth aircraft known as the Horten HIX V3. It was followed in the late 1940s by the Northrop Corporation YB-49 Flying Wing. These aircraft produced a rather low radar signature. Northrop had the lead in stealth technology and eventually won the contract. I am proud to have my father's Northrop Corp 40-year-old model of the B-2.

The Germans were pioneers in precision guided weapons. They employed a radio guided anti-ship missile known as the Fritx X. It was fired from a Dornier 217K-2S bomber against shipping and radio-guided to its target. Its greatest success was against the Italian battleship Roma which sought to escape from Italy to an Allied base. Two missiles were fired and guided to their targets at over 700 miles per hour. Both struck the ship killing 1,400 Italian sailors. The United State began using "smart bombs" late in the Vietnam war to destroy heavily defended bridges from a distance.

Again, "necessity is the mother of invention" as smart bombs were developed due to the high cost of aircraft needed to destroy a bridge in North Vietnam. The need to fly into enemy airspace and return created the necessity for stealth aircraft.

In 1963, my father was invited to join his Air Force buddies led by Don Hillman to Seattle's Gold Unlimited Hydroplane Races. General LeMay's former pilot Russ Schleah was the "Top Unlimited Driver 1956", yet he was still serving on active duty in the Air Force. The result was that many of the old "fly boys" traveled to Lake Washington in

Seattle to watch their comrade compete. It was great to see so many of my dad's buddies and my old SAC Brat mate Stevie. Steve and I were early teenagers and enjoyed going out water skiing on our own on his father's boat on Lake Washington. Steve apparently mellowed out as I guessed I had. There was an absence of dealing with raw eggs, smoke bombs, and when I woke up in the morning my hand was not placed in a bowl of warm water. It is wonderful when you have a friend that you may not have seen for years, you visit and it feels like you have just left. He was always a great guy to hang out with.

Steve dropped by our Palos Verdes home a few years later with his father and Steve's new wife. I think he was around 18. While I was looking forward to going to college, Steve was married and had joined the Air Force as an enlisted airman. I thought my buddy's life was over. He married into a circumstance that presented serious responsibilities in the face of minimal income. I was not mature enough to deal with that.

A few years later Steve was not only an officer but a medical doctor. When I visited him 40 years later, Steve was happily married to the same women and a respected doctor in Sequim, Washington. I thought I played it smart and got my BS and MBA at the University of Southern California but I had two failed marriages by age 39. It makes you wonder about our paths in life.

My father also suffered through two divorces. During the second, we were invited to share Thanksgiving dinner with our dear friends, the Cattons. General Catton, now a three-star officer, commanded SAC's 15th Air Force. General Catton and his wife Jo Beth lived with their son, Jackie, in the impressive 15th Air Force command personal headquarters at March Air Force Base in Riverside, California.

There were several vintage photos of Five-Star General Hap Arnold in General Catton's office. General Arnold led the massive development of the Army Air Corp during World War II. General Arnold was the first and only Five-Star Army Air Force General. After the war, he led the drive in the formation of an independent United States Air Force. General Catton, my father, Jackie and I went out front to toss the football. I played high school football but was slow. Jackie was like a rocket. I could not cover him, and he could catch almost anything his father tossed. Jackie Catton would go to the Air Force Academy. He had a brilliant career retiring as a Major General.

After getting my MBA at Southern Cal, my start as an Investment Advisor was as a stockbroker. It's funny but when you sit at your desk as a new broker, no one calls you to ask your advice or make a transaction. Imagine that! In those days, you could make cold calls and since I represented a reputable firm, Dean Witter Inc., later absorbed by Morgan Stanley folks, might listen to me for a minute. I would make cold calls every weeknight from my office located in Newport Beach, California. The calls were from 7:00 PM to 9:00 PM to avoid interrupting someone's dinner or bedtime. I was using what was called a "reverse directory". It listed phone numbers according to the street. I knew the wealthier neighborhoods of Newport Beach which allowed me to target prospects in affluent homes. The listings had the addresses, names and numbers. I was working a street on my phone, and the next name was Curtis LeMay. I thought there was no way this guy was going to be General Curtis LeMay, but I gave him a call.

A gruff voice answered the phone. I explained what I was doing and then asked him if he was General LeMay. He answered the affirmative and I told him I was Colonel Richard Evans' son. His response was to say, "How is the old boy? Have him give me a call." Further into the conversation, which I respectfully kept brief, and he likely wanted even briefer, I told him that I used to live by his street. He did not know what I was talking about. I said, "as a kid I lived next to LeMay Way in Bellevue, Nebraska". He laughed at the old memory.

I am told I met the great General in person twice. At age five, I handed him a ski rope handle at Lake Carroll as my mom was teaching him to double ski. At age 40, I attended with my wife, Machelle, a book signing in his honor in a home in Nellie Gale, California. His signature in his book *Iron Eagle* given to my father follows:

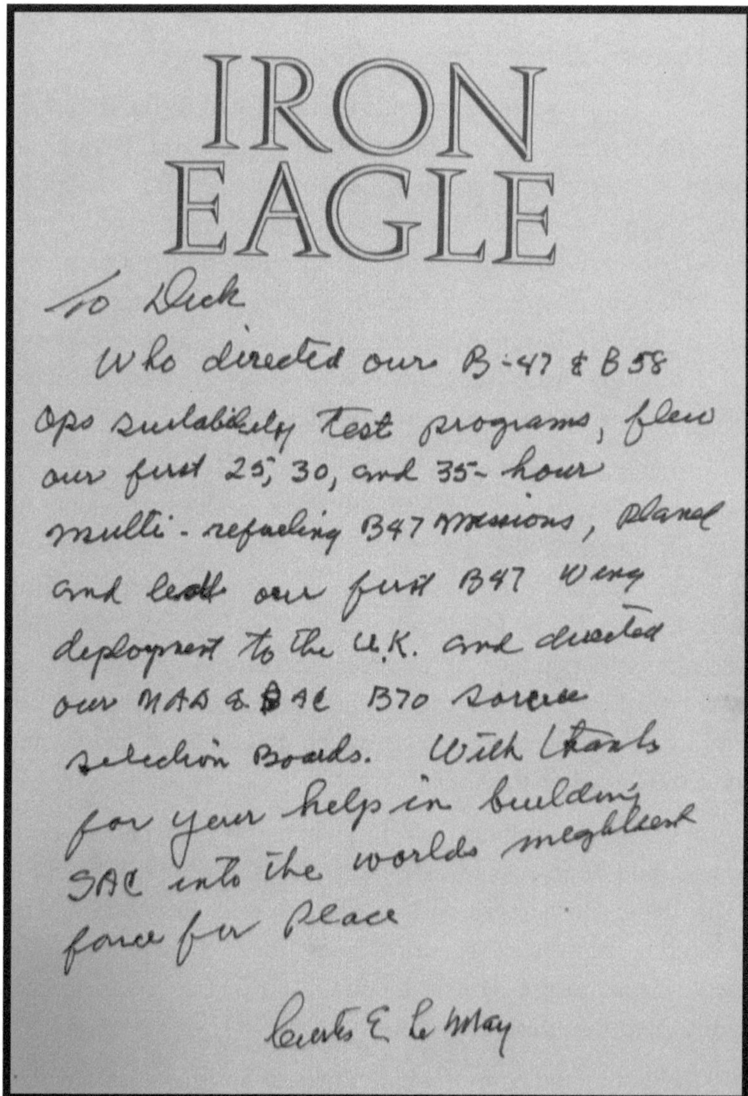

IRON
EAGLE

To Dick

Who directed our B-47 & B58 Ops suitability test programs, flew our first 25, 30, and 35-hour multi-refueling B47 missions, planned and led our first B47 wing deployment to the U.K. and directed our MAD & BAE B70 source selection Boards. With thanks for your help in building SAC into the worlds mightiest force for peace

Curtis E. LeMay

Military men are my heroes. Rich men, great athletes and politicians are of virtually no gravity worthiness to me. Actors are just actors. They are entertaining.

I learned a painful lesson when my mother left my father. This type of event may have subconscious effects on a young man. My mother has rejected my father for another. As a general hypothesis, women are attracted to males with power and the lifestyle and security they can provide. There are different types and degrees of power.

To have a happy secure family as a man, I had to build a nest so to speak. I sought freedom and power. On the one hand, I could acquire the power of money and social influence or earn the raw power of leadership, being tested by danger, adventure and the conquest of a machine. I observed at that time in America, women were so well protected that our people took military service for granted. I chose not to apply to the Air Force Academy, not knowing if I would even be selected. I selfishly made the conscious decision to chase money in the hope it would bring greater personal freedom.

I did not want to work for a goal, and then have it snatched away as I reasoned my father's career had been. With hindsight I realize dreams are arbitrarily lost to civilians as well as service personnel. Emerson was correct in stating that "men live lives of quiet desperation." I chose the safer, well-traveled path. I did have the guts to build my own business and thus not be dependent on another. In some ways, this is a gutsier move than working in a life career with a guaranteed paycheck in the government. It is not close, however, compared to military men and women at the "head of the spear."

A "Lifer" in the military working in supply to get a retirement paycheck should be respected. However, he is not the same person that flies highly dangerous aircraft and is willing to walk away out of principle, literally within months of securing guaranteed, hard earned, lifetime retirement. He is not the same as a young Marine that kicks open a door in Iraq in Operation Desert Storm.

In 1970 I graduated from the University of Southern California. I had the opportunity to join an Air Force Reserve unit at Norton Air Force Base in San Bernadino, California. The Vietnam War was winding down so President Nixon organized a draft based on a drawing of numbers. My draft number was high at 229, which meant I would not be called in. I could now go on to graduate school. Meanwhile, thousands of my contemporaries had not been able to take advantage of the college deferment, had served and some were killed in defense of our nation.

The choice before me was pure and simple. Avoid military service by immediately enrolling in graduate school? The SAC Brats in me "marched" me to Norton AFB where I swore an oath to the Constitution. That was the least I could do. My active reserve squadron, the 61st Aerial Port Squadron, was not called up to active duty although contemporary reserve aerial ports were recalled for nearly two years in response to the 1973 Israeli Egyptian War. I never regretted the six years I spent in the service and never felt in danger. I was in more danger and remain prouder to be Colonel Richard Evans SAC Brat living on an Air Force Base during the Cold War.

Airman Evans with fellow airmen

My father spent six years of his young life training and then immediately being thrown into direct military combat. That heroic phase was followed by a five-years civilian break only to return for an additional eleven years' service.

Reserve Aerial Port squadron missions paralleled the missions of their active-duty aerial port squadrons, dealing with cargo processing, passenger services, fleet service and air terminal operations center controllers. That is all I did for six years in the reserves with only a year's total active duty. No one ever shot at me. With no major war over the last twenty years, my son has spent zero time in the military. It is true that in history that "much is asked of one generation and to another much is given."

I have been blessed to have grown up surrounded by many family members that were fine officers and patriots serving our country valiantly. There was my grandfather Jean Nelson who served in World War I as a pilot and World War II as an engineer in England. Tom Law, my stepdad, who was a Landing Signal Officer (LSO), used signal flags to guide Naval aircraft on final approach preparing to touch down on the dangerous flight decks of the aircraft carriers USS Antietam and USS Bennington. My uncle Tom Evans, who was an Air Corps bomber pilot in the Burma Theatre. My uncle, Colonel Bill (Pug) Evans, was a career Air Force pilot. Uncle John Evans was a navigator in the B-24 bomber. My uncle Joe Wallace was a Lieutenant Colonel in the United States Army Reserves.

Ensign Tom Law on aircraft carrier Antietam

Future Lt Colonel Joe Wallace at graduation ceremony

Lt Jean Nelson in World War I uniform

Captain Jean Nelson in World War II uniform

PART FOUR: HISTORY, CYCLES, AND MARKETS

Chapter 17: The World After the Cold War

Our country defeated communism, at least for a while. The height of the Cold War in the 1950s and 1960s was likely the peak of America power when compared to the rest of the world as was the apex of our people's living standard compared to other nations. Our power and manufacturing abilities are more limited today. The American and European dominated G-7 produces 32 percent of the world's goods and services while the BRICS nations produce 40 percent. BRICS is an intergovernmental organization comprising eleven countries: Brazil, China, South Africa, Egypt, Ethiopia, India, Indonesia, Iran, Russia, Saudi Arabia, and the UAE. Roughly speaking, this means the mother countries in the colonial system now produce less than their former colonies or nations they dominated. The rise of the BRICS nations from the Third World is a revolutionary change in the world's balance of power on a level with the European Age of Exploration in the 15th century.

Napoleon once said of China, "Let China sleep, for when she awakes, she will shake the world."

As a SAC Brat I quietly listened to the ideas of men focused on their responsibility in sustaining the geopolitical power of our nation. Most individuals with a liberal mind set would judge the kinetic methods, selectively necessary to sustain international balance, were brutal. The central premise was that, while desirable but not reality, nations do not maintain peace by being understanding and communicating well with one's neighbors. Nations like a lion pride must be so strong that the hyena never crosses into the pride's lands or threaten its residence. Deterrence was, and is, the key. The Strategic Air Command logo is exactly to the point. A mailed fist holding an olive branch, declaring "Peace is our Profession."

Eleanor Roosevelt, an early supporter of the formation of world ruling bodies such as the League of Nations and United Nations, would be saddened by the results. They have proved to be bankrupt regarding the goal of establishing world peace. Those forums might have been effective if backed by traditionally recognized foundations of established power- diplomatic, economic and military. The floundering United Nations, lacking the credibility being available of soft or hard power, is a debating society.

Nations that rise to power over time are weakened by their increasing success. As nations continue to rise, they tend to overcompensate to challenge the existing power. Their shift can be controlled and somewhat managed as in the case of the United States and Britain. More often the change is violent as in the case of Rome and Carthage in the Punic Wars, Britain and France in the 17th and 18th century, or Germany and Britain in the 20th century.

My father, Colonel Richard Evans, and I grew up in a world in which our nation with its relatively high population, industrial prowess and advantageous geographic position on the earth, could dominate that earth. That time is changing as the colonial children of the European Mother countries have industrialized in the face of huge population growth. The overcompensation of their position has resulted in dynamic growth mirroring European growth during the Age of Exploration and the Industrial Revolution. Geographic location, while still important, is not as dynamic due to rapid transportation having the effect of shrinking the earth.

Though the prior communist nations China, Russia, and Vietnam are employing capitalistic methods to incentivize production, communism remains a threat. Karl Marx wrote the *Communist Manifesto* and *Das Kapital* after the 1840s great depression. Marx was likely impressed by the events he was witnessing and concluded that the proletariat or workers would revolt and bring down the system. He thought that the worker in Russia had more in common with the workers in America or Germany then the workers in Russia had with their employers. Marx discounted the power of nationalism and the universal love of one's nation.

The world economy, instead of continuing its collapse in the 1840s, cycled back into relative prosperity in the years to follow. In the 1890s the economy again fell into a depression and then cycled back. This process repeated following the 1930s depression. After this depression began its recovery, some communists concluded that they had to find a more effective means of taking advantage of economic calamity to bring on the workers revolution they so dearly wanted. Capitalism seemed to have an ability to experience economic chaos, adapt to the new reality and yet recover and provide more benefits. Capitalism and nationalism would modify in each depression, preventing in most cases the conditions necessary for Marx's dreamed of revolt.

A school of thought developed arguing the way communists could bring down a capitalistic system was by creating divisions within society. An example of a divided society in the early 20th century was the Ottoman Empire particularly in the Balkans. The people spoke many different languages, there were numerous nationalities including Italian, German, Croatian, Greek, Hungarian, Romanian and Turkish. The result was many different customs. There were four main religions-Catholicism, Greek Orthodox, Judaism and Islam. The Balkans peninsula was criss-crossed by mountains making it harder for people to travel. Some people wanted to be ruled by a king, some wanted to have democracy, and some wanted the Sultan to continue to rule.

The result was an extremely divided region which gave rise to the expression "Balkanization". The lack of common interest manifests itself in terrible atrocities committed among the varied people against each other during the two World Wars. When Henry Kissinger wrote his book about the lessons of Prince Metternich of the Austro-Hungarian Empire, Kissinger focused on the divided nature of the region and thus the difficulty in ruling it.

The *Bible* tells the story of how mankind became arrogant and built a great structure to reach the sun called the Tower of Babble. To teach mankind a lesson, God gave mankind many languages. The men could not communicate and the society broke down. I think that the less people have in common in a nation, the more vulnerable the nation to civil war.

While the United States history was a story of massive immigration, part of that narrative was about efforts made to Americanize our new citizens. The idea being to unite the people. People were encouraged to learn English and American history. My family background is Norwegian, French, Welsh, German and English. My ancestors came to

America and learned English. The message was optimistic with hope, and great pride in American history and its accomplishments. They thought they were building a great nation and they did.

A school of Marxist social thought developed in the 1920s and 1930s, centered at the University of Frankfurt in Germany. Its theorists sought the end of capitalism and were sharply critical of the traditional social structures — among them the family, patriarchy, the nation, and inherited authority — that they believed sustained it. This became known as the Frankfurt School. Among its notable figures were Carl Grünberg, Felix Weil, Max Horkheimer, Theodor Adorno, Erich Fromm, Herbert Marcuse, and Leo Löwenthal. When the Nazis came to power, the members of the Frankfurt School left Germany. Many moved to the United States and established themselves as professors at Columbia University, where the group was also known as the Institute for Social Research.

It seems to this SAC Brat that the practical effect of the Frankfurt School's thinking was a kind of "divide and conquer" — in the name of greater freedom, the groups within a society are encouraged to turn against one another, weakening the bonds that hold a nation together. Among the traditional targets of this thinking, in my view, were the family and established authority.

Let me give some examples. Since the Presidency of Lyndon Johnson, the government has employed policies that result in dividing of the American people. The government will provide money to a mother if a husband leaves his children. The result has been to discourage marriage, which hurts children. The nation allows voting in numerous languages removing a strong incentive for immigrants to learn a common language English. The development of so-called sanctuary cities and states has the effect of violating Federal law and creating nations within the United States. Until recently, the borders of the United States not protected from mass immigration of millions of people, most of whom have little education and do not speak English. Does this practice divide or unify our nation?

The United States population of approximately 350 million people is about the level of India in 1930. Do we want India's population in 80 years? When does America have enough people?

The media, entertainment and advertising industries produce an unusual number of narratives in which the white male, which represents most American men, is depicted as less intelligent than his wife, minorities or even his children. In narratives, conservative white males are overly depicted as evil. The terrible history of slavery in narratives ignores that slavery has existed for thousands of years, all races have been enslaved, that during the trans-Atlantic slave trade the United States absorbed 5 percent of the total and that the majority of black slaves were in slavery within Africa by black African Kingdoms or Muslim states. Hollywood further ignores that white Europeans were the leaders in ending the slave trade and ending slavery. The British can be very proud for they led this fight to end slavery and were soon joined by the French. The United States after the Civil War fought against slavery while most of Africa, and parts of the Middle East, India and China still had slaves.

Our educational system, dominated by the Teacher's Union, seems to this observer to give generous coverage of America's sins but less credit for her accomplishments. If a minority student is taught that he or she is handicapped by an unfair system with "white privilege" that person will likely react in two ways. They will be angry at their country and European Americans. They will be discouraged from doing their best and working hard to achieve freedom and a wonderful life in this country. Acting like a victim never got anybody success. Overcompensating for a handicap brings success. The victimhood mentality is a rejection of overcompensation, and I continue to argue that ultimately overcompensation is what made Europe able to lead the world for almost 400 years. The victim hood mentality divides our people for if there is a victim there must be a predator and the media seems to indicate that predator is the white man. The same men that industrialized the world, built rockets to go to the moon, defeated innumerable diseases, developed the ideas of a republic and personal freedom, and yes ended slavery.

The mental view at Strategic Air Command was that if you had an obstacle or problem then solve it. Don't make excuses or blame others.

America has gotten away from that way of thinking, and it shows in our accelerating decline in power and our people's living standards.

The media narrative does not seem to explain the positive contributions made by Europeans to fight the plague of slavery. It is estimated that slavery has reappeared in the millions within sub-Sahara Africa in black nations. If one group is responsible for ending the slavery plague, then why does the media narrative attack that group as if they were the sole perpetrators of the crime? Is it an effort to divide our people against each other?

The history of America has many skeletons in its closet. There are many things to be ashamed of but on the whole Americans have so much to be proud off. A media that dwells on the negative without including the far greater positive of our history cannot be proud of its behavior. Is this behavior influenced by the Frankfort School of Thought?

What I do know is in the last forty years, our nation has spent trillions to bring justice to our people, yet the nation seems so divided. I think many of the policies I have mentioned are important factors.

Note that the battle between nationalism and almost a diverse internationalistic nihilism is an echo of the bloody fight between Stalin and Trotsky and on a more civilized level between Woodrow Wilson and Senator Lodge. In the event the world experiences a depression, I expect there will likely be a greater struggle between these forces.

Men are biological beings and our systems and institutions are likely more biological then intellectual then we care to admit. More research needs to be done on the Kondratieff Wave and the effects of climate change on human history. There are numerous examples in history of the former slavish peoples becoming masters. The Germans' conquest of Rome, the Arab destruction of the Byzantine Empire, the Russian pushback of the Tartars are examples. Will BRICS lead the G-7 and America someday?

During the Cold War, the United States avoided direct conflict with the major Eurasian powers until we concluded our interests were in danger. When we entered the Eurasia wars of the 20th century, we acted in a manner that tended to ensure that our country would be on the winning side. We were late joining both World Wars to our great advantage. Americans believe that both wars were clear moral issues and joining the Allies meant being on the moral high ground. But is this completely true? Is that argument used to justify the sacrifices made? Were the results of World War I positive? In World War II were our allies the Communist Soviet Union superior to Nazi Germany? Did America remove Japan as an adversary and replace it with China? Politics does make strange bedfellows.

With hindsight it seems that Roosevelt's policies were genius. He waited until the Germans and Russians had destroyed millions of each other's soldiers, the British were bankrupt, and the Japanese over extended and Roosevelt then maneuvered the Axis into attacking the United States. Our nation then paid a relatively low price in blood to weaken our potential enemies and inherited a great deal of the benefits of the European Empires.

Churchill, Halifax and Chamberlain in contrast urged the British to defend a fascist Poland against a fascist Germany that wanted Danzig, a German Hanseatic city back. It had been a German city for 500 years. They managed to get their country in a war with a Germany that would have likely attacked the communist Soviet Union in the future and avoided war with the West. The British and French could have waited patiently as Roosevelt did for the war to spread to the Soviet Union weakening both their country's potential enemies Germany and Russia. Then after completing the bankruptcy of the British Empire and ignoring obvious Soviet abuses Churchill discovered that Soviet Communism was a danger and told the world about the "Iron Curtain." Was Churchill asleep in the 1920s and 30s as Stalin killed millions? Did any leader believe that the Soviets did not commit mass murder of millions of Ukarainians during the Five-Year Plans and the Katyn massacres of Poles in 1940?

In the Cold War the United State viewed itself as being so powerful that it sometimes was the first nation in the fray. With the exception of the Chinese in Korea, we avoided potential Eurasian conflict with any major powers. With the change in manufacturing power over the last 50 years, the United States is not as powerful as our leaders seem to think. The result is that in the time of the BRICS nations the United States should be more reluctant to get into conflicts outside our still very large spere of influence, the Western Hemisphere.

Note the difficulty the United States has today in dealing with Iran, a regional power. In 1941-45 the British and Russians invaded the neutral Iran needing only 80,000 troops. According to the United States State Department, Iran's population was 15 million prior to the British and Russian occupation. The Allies took control of the Iranian railroads and 80% of the trucks to facilitate the transporting of Lend Lease from the Persian Gulf to the Soviet Union. A famine resulted and the population of Iran fell according to the State Department to 10-12 million people. Iran a nation that was neutral in the Second World War was invaded and the result was the loss of up to 33 percent of its people. It is likely that Iran lost on a percentage basis more of its population due to World War II than any other nation. It is a disgrace that our media has zero to little coverage of this atrocity committed on the Iranian people as we debate how our nation should deal with that nation.

Now Iran's population is approaching 100 million. The technological gap between the dominant nations of the 20th century and the former colonies or third world has shrunk. Can the West treat Iran as a weak nation anymore?

It is essential to have strong allies in Eurasia if we are to have military influence in that region. General Douglas MacArthur was correct to advise that the United States avoid Asian land wars. The United States needs to keep it simple in this complex world. Our nation must identify America's major economic and security rivals and then focus on balancing power versus that potential adversary.

The obvious rival is China. Chinese weakness in the 19th and 20th century is an anomaly. That situation is truly a historic exception to the rule for China. The most recent official 2025 National Defense Strategy defines "China as by far the pacing threat against which United States forces must prepare, while Russia is evaluated as a well-armed nuclear Rogue state, secondary but dangerous. China is well on its way to fielding robust space-based targeting systems that threaten each of our land and sea-based assets at sea and on the ground. We must acquire counter-space systems at scale or China will be capable of targeting all United

States assets with impunity and in real time within the foreseeable future." China is clearly an exception.

How can the United States offset the Chinese challenge? First identify nations that are most endangered by China and harmonize a united front. The three most powerful countries fearing China are Japan, India and Russia. While the United States has no border dispute with China, Japan, India and Russia do. The nation with the most acute dispute with China is Russia. China's sweeping claims of sovereignty over the South China Sea have antagonized competing claimants Brunei, Indonesia, Malaysia, the Phillipines, Taiwan and Vietnam.

During the 19th century the Russians made territorial agreements with China that the Chinese call the "Unequal Treaties." The result was that a weak China forfeited to Russia almost one million square miles of Siberian territory. Just as China demands the return of Taiwan, China wants the eventual return of the territories lost to Russia. The solution is that the United States needs to recognize Russian interests in the Ukraine and take the role as an arbitrator between Russia and China. Some may call this an effort to play one nation off against the other as Theodore Roosevelt did with Japan in the Russo Japanese War or Nixon with his "Ping pong diplomacy." They would be right to assume that.

Taiwan remains the stumbling block for the United States and China. Particularly if America seeks a role as an arbitrator for Asia. The first step, which appears to be taken, is to diversify computer chip production to the United States away from Taiwan. Unless our military believes that the United States can defeat a billion people fighting 100 miles from their coast and 6,000 miles from ours at a reasonable cost, we might consider appeasing the Chinese.

Taiwan reminds me of the Czechoslovakia crisis and the Munich Agreement in 1938. There was no question that if the American concept of self-determination was to be applied as our own President Woodrow Wilson selectively claimed, then Germany had a right to the Sudetenland. The people in that area were German and wanted to join Germany. The Germans pressured the remaining Czechoslovakian government to allow the occupation of Moravia. The Westen Allies might have ignored this, though ethnic Germans were not the majority in this region. Germany was not alone in occupying the nation that was created by the Versailles Treaty 19 years before. The Hungarians and Poles also took portions of Moravia.

The murder of a German diplomat by a young Jewish man in Paris resulted in an eruption of a German pogrom against Jewish Germans that rivaled outrages of the Middle Ages. The Kristallnacht riots resulted in dozens of innocent Jewish deaths and millions in property damage throughout Germany. The German government then forced the Jewish community to pay for the damage. The English and French public were so disgusted that their nations hardened their foreign policy toward Germany. The result was the end of appeasement and an Allied unsympathetic position concerning Germany's arguably legitimate claim to the return to the Reich of German Danzig from Poland.

The loss of Czechoslovakia was a tremendous blow for the French as 35 Czechoslovakian army divisions and all the excellent Czechoslovakian equipment were either removed from the Allies' ledger or absorbed by the German. Most importantly the Skoda munitions plants went to the German side. One could argue that overall, the Munich Agreement was reasonable considering "self-determination" and perhaps necessary, but it completely upset the balance of power in Europe and led to the start of World War II.

Few would argue that China does not have a historic claim to Taiwan. Didn't the Japanese Empire fight a war with Chian and take the territory? It is simple. The 1820 to 1948 time in China is an aberration in weakness in Chinese history. The Chinese government wants Taiwan back and there is some justice in that argument. Do we want to risk a war with a major power over a stolen province that nation wants returned? We even recognize Taiwan as a province of China.

Unless the United State divests its interests in Taiwan in the computer chip area, the loss of that regions production capacity to China might be comparable to the acquisition of the Skoda Industrial plants to Germany in 1938-39. If the United States lost a conventional war over Taiwan, it would shatter the balance of power in Asia as the Munich crisis aftermath did to Europe. If the United States abandons Taiwan, perhaps that will upset the balance of power in Asia. Taiwan is likely the most dangerous issue in the world.

If the civilian and military leadership in the United States view Taiwan as indefensible or not worth the blood and treasure necessary to defend, we should consider doing what the British did in 1867 with the United States. The British gave us what we wanted. We should strongly consider settling the issue in Taiwan in China's favor. Perhaps a quid pro quo could be negotiated for no Chinese or Russian interference in our removing the current leadership in Cuba in return the United States would not interfere in China's Taiwanese issues and Russian Donbas claims. In short, to respect each nation's historic spheres of influence and remove a casa bellum.

Unless we take a proactive stance on Taiwan and remove the confusion over whether we will defend the island or not, we are asking for trouble. It would be far better for the United States to negotiate a multiyear transfer of power of Taiwan to China as if it was our idea than to have a crisis with China and be forced to go to war or be humiliated and forced to back down. A crisis with China in which we are threatened in some ways could cause the United States to dig in its heel and have greater risk of a war we would likely lose.

India is a natural ally of America. India's number one problem is Pakistan and the Muslim states. India is vulnerable to the loss of Russian and Middle Eastern oil. Indians are aware of the importance of the Straits of Malacca and Singapore as the dividing line of Chines and Indian power. India wants to make sure that the Indian Ocean remains secure as the Indian Ocean.

Japan off the coast of Asia like Britain continues to endure as possibly the United States most valued and trustworthy ally (except Australia) Japan's history records this nation as being constantly tested and threatened.

China continues to exert intense pressure on Japan in the East China Sea, characterized by frequent, aggressive incursions around the Senkaku Island that China attempts to claim as its historic territory.

In some ways modern China is like 18th and early 19th century France. Both were the most powerful and populous nations on their continents. Both nations had an adversary with a powerful navy secure on an island of the coast. Both nations' power was balanced by a combination of other neighboring continental powers and the offshore nation carefully deciding when to intervene to maintain that balance. The United States should follow the British example.

Prior to World War I, the Germans worked with the Ottoman Empire to build the Berlin to Baghdad railroad. The British were able to delay completion until prior to World War II. The Germans wanted the railroad to allow access to the Persian Gulf and the oil resources in the region. While it was more expensive to ship oil via the railroad verses a ship, the Germans knew that in the event of war with the British Empire, the Suez Canal would be closed to German shipping and thus Persian Gulf oil supplies could not reach Germany. The British Navy, which was the most powerful in the world at that time, could stop German naval movement of oil.

The Chinese face a similar problem. In the event of war with the United States, the Chinese would face the United States Navy and the Western control of the Malacca Straits near Singapore as a blocking force preventing Chinese access to the Indian Ocean and the Persian Gulf oil. The Chinese solution is to build a rail line, road and pipeline from China to Russian oil fields, Middle East and to Europe itself. It is known as the Belt and Road Initiative (BRI). This is an echo of the German plan and illustrates how geography has a profound effect on spending and infrastructure. Both the Berlin to Baghdad railroad and the Belt and Road Initiative are designed to maintain oil supplies despite an oceanic choke point and a superior enemy navy.

It is fascinating that the issue of trade between Europe and Asia remains a major concern today just as in the 15th century, the beginning of the Age of Exploration.

A second possibility for increased America power is the annexation of portions of Canada and exerting greater influence in Greenland, although they currently offer unrestricted geographic United States access. We should consider reestablishing our strong relationship with Iceland to establish our American presence again after we withdrew our long-established U.S. Navy P-3 patrol squadrons and the Air Force fighter Interceptor squadron from Keflavik IAP. Several provinces in Canada have more in common with the western U. S. then Ottawa. Quebec, given her citizen's demand that Canada, as a nation, adhere to the bi-lateral French English as the official language, could present a challenge. With or without some union, Canada and the U. S. have a common fear of rising China. The two nations share a common language and traditions and should continue their outstanding coordination within North American Air Defense Command (NORAD) as United State Air Force and Royal Canadian Air Force pilots do today, flying wingtip to wingtip, intercepting Russia Tu-95MS long-range bombers off the coast of Alaska. Australia, with its first-class defense posture and weapons, and New Zealand, whose defense posture is the opposite of Australia's, also will have common cause due to common language and culture with America. Both like America being islands.

America should treat Europe as in the Napoleonic Wars, World War I and World War II at arm's length. While historians argue that America could have prevented World War II, I would argue against this view. America prospered and paid a far lower price in blood by being late for these wars. Our geography allows United States leadership greater time to analyze the situation. My opinions are often in agreement with the views stated by Pat Buchanan in his excellent book *Hitler Churchill and the Unnecessary War.*" I suspect George Washington would agree as well.

Russia will likely be an ally superior to European nations in a United States versus China scenario. The reason is again geography since Russia and China share a several thousand-mile border. Conversely, Russia might be a danger with the possibility of Russia dragging the United States into an unnecessary war with China.

America being an island enjoys the strategic luxury of geographic isolation, aloof and therefore remaining above the fray in Eurasian conflicts until after the participants offer the United States a situational advantage to tip the scales. America can choose the winning side. America will not have the power and will to waste its tremendous geographic advantage, preventing nations outside our hemisphere, like Israel, to drag us into their conflicts.

What is the future of Israel? The idea of a Jewish homeland was born during a time of relatively high European populations versus the Ottoman Empire. The technological gap between the European nations and the Turks was vast. Most Jews were working to become respected citizens of their host nations. Most Jews were not Zionists and thus were not in favor of the formation of a Jewish state in Palestine. This is akin to the fact that most Catholics did not support the Papacy controlling large areas of Italy in the 19th century.

Judaism like Papal Catholicism during the time of Garibaldi will likely be a religion and not a homeland or state.

Zionists argued the only safety for the Jewish people was to possess their own nation and territory. Many Christians were Zionist for they thought the formation of Israel was a step toward the "return of Christ". The Zionist movement was born in Europe, led by European Jews, in the age of European power and overseas colonization. Are they an echo of the European Crusades? Is Israel the last great European colony?

These questions ultimately do not matter since in the jungle among nations "might makes right". Arguing over "stolen land" as if there was an ultimate owner of a territory is strictly a function of where one thinks history begins. I find it unreasonable when a Mexican U. S. citizen claims Texas was "stolen" from Mexico. Didn't the Mexican's steal the land from the Spanish who stole it from the Indian tribes that occupied the area at the time? Didn't that Indian tribe steal the land from other tribes over a conflict lasting since time began? Texas is unique in this chain for the Mexicans and Spanish never really settled most of Texas because the Comanches prevailed in retaining control to the Indians for 100 years.

Human history on a national scale has always reminded me of the struggle of lion prides to control hunting territories. One group replaces the other and then they are replaced. The defining issue is power. They don't "steal land". They destroy the present occupier of the land or drive the occupants away. Nations behaved in the same manner and, in extreme cases, committed genocides.

The Zionist accumulated the power and empathy to form the state of Israel in 1948. The Arabs and Palestinians were relatively weak. The world sympathized and supported the suffering of Jews following World War II

. Upon witnessing European nations turning on their Jewish citizens during the war, the mass of Jews finally agreed with the Zionist argument that Jewish security mandated a Jewish State. Security for the Jewish state was reinforced by the many Zionists who had received military training during the war.

In Britain, France, and the United States, organized political support for Israel — rooted in post-war sympathy and active domestic constituencies — helped move those governments to provide financial, military, and political aid to the newly established State of Israel. Israel quickly cemented a technological advantage over her Arab opponents. That advantage, combined with Israeli military audacity, secured victory in the 1956 Suez Canal War and the 1967 War, which considerably expanded Israel's borders. The shrinking gap between Arab and Israeli power was in evidence in the more closely run 1973 war.

Israeli's 1973 war affected me as my Air Lift Command Element (ALCE) was almost called to active duty. The war was short and ended in another Israeli victory. It is rumored that the Israelis considered using nuclear weapons. Egypt's early gains, however, eventually led to the return of the Sinai Peninsula through the 1979 peace treaty.

Peace was negotiated by Jimmy Carter at Camp David by guaranteeing an annual fixed foreign aid stipend to each of the three participants, approximately three billion dollars to Israel, sixty percent of Israel's annul stipend to Egypt and a lesser amount to Jordan. The agreement remains in place today although the top line has increased.

Paying tribute to adversaries is a normal step taken by a declining power. During the late years of the Roman Empire, Attila the Hun demanded payments of between 700 and 2,000 pounds of gold per year to not invade the Eastern Roman Empire. When the United States was a young nation, Muslim Barbary Pirates would attack European and American ships unless an annual payment was made. Many nations just paid tribute. The United States eventually built a navy to destroy the piracy "on the shores of Tripoli."

Years later the French Directory demanded that each of its corrupt members be paid $50,000 plus a $10 million loan to be made to France by the United States. In return, the French promised to not attack or capture American merchant ships during the Napoleonic Wars. Our battle cry was a toast stating, "Millions for defense but not one cent for tribute." Has the modern United States become more like the Roman Empire during its later years?

The Palestinian leader Yasser Arafat stated that the Palestinians would recover their lands from the Jews via the Palestinian women's womb. He was saying what Nixon stated. Nixon reasoned that Israel's long-term problem was the high Arab birth rate. Higher birth rates are also the problem of the Mother Countries, and the United States versus the former colonies or Third World. In some ways the original colonial masters sowed the seeds of their weakness and possible destruction by compassionately improving the lives of the people in their colonies. Europeans should get credit for extending life expectancies, medical care and food production in their former colonies. The result is a growing extreme imbalance in the populations. With many nations becoming overpopulated which contributes to military power how does that affect the world? When will there be to many people?

Time is not on Israel's side. There are three problems facing the Jewish state. First, the Arab population transiting in and out of Israel is overtaking the Israel state. Second, the technological gap between first and third world nations has diminished. Third, Israel depends on American power to do the heavy military lifting for Israel at a time when American military and economic power is declining relative to the Third World. While America can reposition its power from Eurasia back to the safety of the American hemisphere, Israel has no ocean moat to protect it.

Trends project that Israel will eventually be absorbed by the Arab human Sea prompting many Jews to immigrate to the United States. If Israel is destined to cycle down, its exit has the potential to be very violent. I am reminded of Israel's nuclear weapons and the story of Samson.

History has many examples of nations in a slow decline extending their power for centuries. The key is to avoid imperial overreach and if possible, use geographic barriers for defense. As the Roman Empire was winding down, its governmental structure and social life was possibly extended due to the efforts of Diocletian. He stabilized the government and organized the frontier along defensible geographic lines. The Rhine River flowing to the North Sea and Danube River flowing to the Black Sea formed the northern border from their starting point high in the Alps. Perhaps Metternich allowed Austro-Hungary another 50 years of power. He was able to organize the monarchies of Europe to assist each other in controlling their restive populations. America requires a leader that understands its relative limits and the ability to manage the decline in American relative power. America has a fantastic advantage with two lovely oceans moats separating us from the masses of humanity. Rome had rivers, deserts, and mountains for defense, Great Britain had the English Channel, while the United States has oceans.

We have a valuable geographic advantage if used effectively.

Chapter 18: Cycles — Kondratieff, Markets, and Tuna Theory

Like Rome in the time of Diocletian, our country is going bankrupt. Most Americans will agree with that view, but they will add that our nation will cleverly "inflate its way out". This means the debts will be paid with less valuable money in the future. The answer for our citizens is to continue to own things with the expectation that they will be more expensive in the future. The result is a speculative mentality which is seen in house prices, stock prices and a greater willingness to gamble than in the past. Fifty years ago, the average American house cost 1.3 times the average income of the family. Now the cost is eight times the average income. The average new automobile transaction amounts to $50,000. Young people cannot afford a home and responsible married couples delay having children for years to save the resources to start a family. The percent of people under 30 living at home with their parents is far above historic levels. The savings rate in America is considerably below the rates for industrial nations. People have a "live for today" viewpoint and therefore want to spend their money on experiences rather than savings. Regrettably, rainy days do come.

Meanwhile Americans with multiple children without a father in the home receive government subsidies necessary to give these children basic food and shelter. In these situations, the government has become the parent supporting the family. The more fatherless children, the greater the government payments. We now have generations of unproductive people whose way of life is to live off the government's charity. We have half a million homeless people living out of tents and shelters for the night collecting disability and food stamp checks so that homelessness is a way of life. Some of this charitable money is then spent on drugs as the homeless endure their miserable lives.

An argument can be made that our nation will simply default on its debt or a large portion and start over. In a system that practices fractional banking, a default would collapse the money supply. The value of the remaining dollars could rise against other assets. Leveraged assets, such as real estate and common stock, would collapse in price.

How could this happen? The government currently spends more than $1.2 trillion annually on debt interest payments. This is likely a low estimate since the debt is approximately $40 trillion and a $1.2 trillion interest payment implies a 2.7% cost of capital. The 10-year government bond pays 4.5%. If the government paid the current rate the annual interest payment would be $1.80 trillion. Part of the reason for the difference is that debt secured at previously lower interest rates has not matured and does not have to be replaced by costlier debt yet. This fact alone represents a potential interest cost time bomb.

A second reason for the disparity is that the government in reporting interest cost sometime leaves out the government bond interest that must be paid the various government trust funds. This is estimated at over 20 percent of the national debt. It has been suggested that in the case of Social Security, military pensions, government worker pensions and Medicare, the interest payments are made to us; therefore, they are sometimes not considered. If this is true, then why don't we exclude interest payments to individual Americans? If they are Americans and own the debt, aren't we just paying it to ourselves? The process appears a bit dishonest in its result of misleading the interest expense cost.

Since the American government cannot balance its budget, the money to pay the interest must be borrowed. At some point, won't the ever-increasing government borrowing result in an interest rate so high that the government cannot collect and borrow enough to pay the interest expense? Any overextended borrower will reach a point at which their lenders will demand a higher interest rate to offset the increased risk of default. This stage paradoxically can accelerate the default.

Wouldn't a president gain greater funds to employ in the government by deciding to stop interest payments on some or all the debt? The government would immediately have that money, not devoted to debt payments, available. Could the payments to families on various welfare systems and the homeless continue to get their full assistant checks? How would they respond? How would the price of houses and stocks respond?

The tendency of books concerning economics, history and war is to have the author summarize and point out what the mistakes were. The idea being that man is rational and can learn from his past mistakes. The Greeks in their myths seem to have a different viewpoint. Their stories are full of narratives concerning a "destiny" known via a prophet's prediction. The human characters do all they can to avoid the predicted result of the gods' will, yet in the end all the results predicted come to pass. One example is Homer's *Iliad* . King Priam is warned that his newborn son Paris will destroy Troy. Priam orders the child killed but the child is sent away and raised by shepherds. The child returns a man, and Priam cannot turn his grown son away. Paris unwittingly proceeds to do what is necessary to destroy Priam's Kingdom.

Aren't the Presbyterian concepts of "predestination" and "free will" the same lesson? The cycles of nature or God know and direct the future, and men have "free will". In the end, the collective "free will" cannot change the result. In the 20th century, could war have been avoided with late industrial nations pushing for a "place in the sun?" If Hitler, Mussolini or Tojo, each possessing free will, had been all killed would that have changed the world's path to war? With diplomacy, production and tactics perhaps, the winner could have been different. But evidence appears the cycles were predestined for war.

Does history indicate that an individual leader can prevent a collision between China and the United States sometime in the next 20 years? Are the odds good?

Does a change in relative power between nations lead to conflict? Can a change in power between a couple increase the odds of divorce? This question reminds me of the song, *Don't You Love Me Baby?*

I fall into the same trap that I criticize. I use mainly the Pat Buchanan arguments concerning World War II and the likelihood that Churchill's strategy was a failure particularly for the British Empire. How can I argue that we are prisoners of fate when I am implying that specific decisions by a leader changed events? Why try to learn from history if conflicts are predestined? Perhaps the answer is that free will is a tool which allows a nation to increase the odds that its side or even genes are the winner if there must be a conflict.

The Russian economist Nicholas Kondratieff 100 years ago proposed a cyclic theory that has affected my father and my life. I think it will influence my children's lives so I will discuss it here. Kondratieff is mentioned favorably in Solzhenitsyn's *Gulag Archipelago,* in the work of Harvard economist Joseph Schumpeter and by Lyndon Johnson's National Security Advisor Walter Rostow. The theory that Kondratieff proposed in my opinion has a fatalistic nature since it views economic history as essentially uncontrollable or as an outcome of fate.

Kondratieff oversaw food production for the Soviet Union under Lenin and was given some credit for predicting the Great Depression in the West. This was in line with Marxism for the communist thought their economic philosophy would be brought into navigating world power by a massive economic collapse followed by a workers' revolt. Kondratieff made the mistake of arguing that the economy was cyclical and that any depression, as bad as it might be, would cycle back to prosperity. Stalin was unhappy with this view for he believed in a "Planned Economy" and from his communist perspective "reason." He seemed to ignore human herding or cycles.

Isn't communism or Marxism the classic view that people are rational and with proper education they will see their errors, learn, and achieve peace and happiness? Kondratieff, with his emphasis on cycles, argued that people are emotional and are influenced by each other or the crowd. The result, according to Solzhenitsyn, was that Kondratieff was purged and died in a labor camp. Per Kondratieff's prediction, the economy cycled back.

There are many interesting analyses of the Kondratieff Wave as it is called. This SAC Brat will do his best to explain the theory as I understand it. I am not a credentialed academic above the MBA level, but I have the scars and insight earned in the trenches as a hedge fund manager in the markets, so my explanation will be simpler. I must state that the theory is controversial and therefore not well known. One possible reason that more economists have not embraced the theory to a greater degree is that Kondratieff makes the argument that ultimately, we do not control the economy. If true, then why train economists to run the economy? Did Kondratieff steal a page from the Greeks and Homer?

The Long Wave or Kondratieff can be divided into three major factors that seem to drive approximately a 54-year or a three generational economic cycle. There is evidence of this cycle going back prior to the Tulip Mania. If one follows the cycle back to the Great Depression of 1932, and recovery beginning in 1949, the economy has avoided depression for over 80 years. Does this mean the 54 year cycle is over?

There are two factors indicating the cycle is still in play. First, the cycle appears to be three generational and life expectancies have gone up considerably since the 1930s. Couples have also delayed the age of having children, which would lengthen the future cycles to accommodate three generations. Second, some argued that the Great Financial Crisis of 2009 was the Kondratieff Depression mitigated by the government. If true, it would be a victory for a planned economy. I agree with the former and not the latter and will make my argument later.

I would argue that the primary factors in the cycle are debt default resulting in deflation, rapid technological innovation, and a toughening up of the general population. There is a tendency to witness a "trough war" in the aftermath of the debt default phase as nations reorganize and establish a balance of power. When I spoke of this at various economic forums, I used the example of dogs of 25 breeds dumped into an indoor basketball court. Initially the dogs will snarl and fight to establish their pecking order of dominance. Once the New Order is established, there is peace with the more powerful animals, granted the nicer locations, perhaps a corner or under the basketball hoop. I believe nations act in the same manner after a debt default and depression.

The 1930s depressionary period resulted in the Japanese pushing for an "East Asia Coprosperity Sphere." The Italian pushed for a "New Roman Empire" and the Germans wanted Lebensraum or "living space." All were aggressive expansionary foreign policies generating "trough wars" with the goal of gaining empire at the expense of the native people and existing colonial powers. These were arguments to get a "place in the sun."

If we travel back from the 1932-49 prewar period, we witnessed the Depressions of the 1870-90s with corporate, railroad and farm debt default. William Jennings Bryan's "Cross of Gold" speech epitomizes the deflationary pressure of this time. Europeans and Americans (Spanish American War) embarked on expansionistic empire building in Africa, Caribbean, Pacific, and Asia during this time.

Travel back to the 1830-40s and we again witness massive debt default focused on Andrew Jackson quarrel with the Bank of the United States. The period is sometimes called the "Hungry Forties". In 1848 and 1854 reflecting the economic chaos, Karl Marx wrote the *The Communist Manifesto* and *Das Kapital.* Any fan of the musical *Les Miserbles* knows of the massive French turmoil in 1848. That same year saw the United States under Manifest Destiny conclude a war with Mexico acquiring California, New Mexico, Arizona, Nevada, parts of Texas and Colorado. Did Manifest Destiny, the idea that America should expand to the Pacific at the expense of the present owners, have goals in common with German “Lebensraum”, the British “The White Man’s Burden” or the Japanese “East Asia Coprosperity Sphere?”

In the 1770s to 1790s the world witnessed massive debt default. The reason for the tax on tea which resulted in the Boston Tea Party was the fact that the East India company was nearing bankruptcy. This was the largest company in the world by far and it was negatively affected by the British Financial Crisis of 1772-73. The tea tax was a subsidy for the company. Interestingly, tea prices were cheaper in the British Colonies then in England due to most of the beverage consumed being smuggled. The source of this tea was from Holland. A weak economy was a factor in the American Revolution. The French government went bankrupt in the 1789 which was the major factor in the French Revolution and Napoleonic Wars.

Fifty odd years earlier in the early 1720s bankruptcies occurred in the two leading economies France and England. Both nations sponsored trading companies. England launched the South Sea Company and France created the Louisiana Company. Both companies went bankrupt. Highly intelligent men such as Sir Isaac Newton lost the equivalent of millions in speculation in the South Sea Bubble. So much for the economic argument of intelligent men ruling their emotions.

Two hundred years later, Winston Churchill, certainly not a dummy and Head of the English Exchequer (Treasury) was destitute in the late 1930s default due to stock speculation. Do our emotions rule us?

There is evidence of a deflation in prices, which implies a debt default and shrinkage of the money supply cycling back to the Magna Carta. The English kept excellent records of wheat prices, a major source of food. The record indicates a 50 to 54-year cycle.

Thomas Jefferson was aware of a cycle from the ***Bible*** called the Jubilee. Every 50 years in the Year of Jubilee all debts were supposedly forgiven and all slaves freed in ancient Israel. This represented an effort to restore equality among the people. Thomas Jefferson argued that the Jubilee cycle should be incorporated into the Constitution to correct excess and avoid the passing on of debt from one generation to the other. He argued for a 19-year cycle or a generational cycle. This had the effect of cutting the jubilee cycle into thirds. Strangely the Mayan calendar, which was cultural and religious, operated on a 52-year cycle. In this case, there is no evidence of debt forgiveness.

The debt default cycle likely serves the function of cleansing the economy of excess and is a form of economic forest fire. Just as the forest fire makes a forest healthy, periodic debt defaults destroy inefficiency, restore discipline, and allows new ideas to more efficiently develop. This view is not acceptable to economists supporting mathematical theories that would allow the economy to be fine-tuned with a Keynesian wrench like an automobile engine. Do these people think men and the crowd are rational?

The clearly successful Theory of Reflexivity, which George Soros gives major credit for his financial success, differ with the view that men are like logical machines. A cornerstone of the theory is that reality creates perception in markets and the economy and that perception creates reality. According to Soros, manias are driven by a bio feedback loop as perception changes what investors think is reality. This is emotionally driven not logically driven. Emotion is clearly identified as animal spirits while logic is more machine like.

Technology is another marker of the Kondratieff Wave Cycle. An alternate approach is based on Joseph Schumpeter's term "creative destruction". This term is used regularly in the highly competitive computer industry. Another term for the same idea is the old expression, "necessity is the mother of invention". In the Kondratieff Wave there is a point in which the technology that runs the economy becomes stagnant. The rates of return drop and leverage is employed to prop up the rate. Debt is built up with the resulting increase in money supply causing higher prices. Higher prices imply necessity. Thus, higher prices create the need to cut consumption and to also look for other answers to the growing scarcity problem. This search results in inventions.

The inventions or technological breakthroughs result in a massive increase in the production of an item that was once scarce. Thus "necessity is the mother of invention." An easy example in our time is horizontal drilling or techniques to develop oil shale. Once prices became too high for the economy, human ingenuity or invention kicked in. Now the United States produces enough oil to supply its needs.

The problem with a technological cycle occurs when demand lags production as the inventions lead to overproduction. Overproduction leads to waiting for the economy to catch up, causing unemployment until the economy can work through the change. The term "creative destruction" makes the point that overproduction destroys highly in-debt industries hampered by old technology.

In general, the technological cycle driving prior waves are the following:

- **1790s** canals and automated textile production utilizing water power
- **1840s** steam engine driving machinery, cotton gins, railroads and steamboats
- **1890s** oil drilling, the Bessemer steel process, internal combustion and turbine engines
- **1930s** electricity, aircraft, autos, radio, rockets, and computers

There are subjective measures of the difference between a recession and a depression. The adage was "a recession was when the husband was unemployed and a depression was when his wife was out of work."

Roughly a recession would see unemployment of 10-15 percent and a depression 25-30 percent with lower wages. A depression should force blue chip stocks to yield 6-10 percent. That reveals a large decline in equity values. Massive debt default is characteristic of depression. The 2009 recession did not have those levels of despair. The government interceded to guarantee key debts while intercepting and stabilizing the system avoiding debt default. Thus, I do not think the world has gone through a depressionary stage in my lifetime.

My understanding of the Kondratieff Wave is that a depression occurs as an economic event. An event in which the prior technology and debt are so powerful that it results in overproduction, massive over capacity, high unemployment and debt default. Companies made inefficient by the revolution in technology go bankrupt. Are we not at risk of that problem in our time with the mania over-artificial intelligence and excess private, corporate and governmental debt?

My first exposure to the Kondratieff Long Wave was reading Robert Beckman's book *The Down Wave,* with its excellent analysis of the bond market which also tracks this cycle. This long-term interest rate chart illustrates tracking a portion of the cycle. While the recent cycle dwarfs the priors, you will note the tendency of cycles to peak every 50-60 years.

Is there a 50–60-year cycle in play here?

I once shared an investment panel with the pioneer of Financial TV Louis Rukeyser, Michael Boskin, head of President George W. Bush's Council of Economic Advisors and Robert Bleiberge the Editorial Editor of *Barrons.* Bleiberg wisely stated, "when you make a price prediction don't give a date."

In keeping with this advice, I predict in the future our nation will experience a debt default at the government and Federal Reserve level. It will be led by a bear market in stocks. It will likely be classified as depression. Nationalism will conflict with internationalism and capitalism challenged by the advocates of the Frankfurt School. The risk of conflict between China and the United States will require the greatest diplomatic skill.

The third factor in the Kondratieff Wave is the strength of the people. This is not Kondratieff's view but the view of this SAC Brat. The expression "shirt sleeve to shirt sleeve in three generations" seems applicable here.

The expression that is sometimes credited to Andrew Carnegie but likely penned by Edward Atkinson (1882) implies that wealth rarely extends beyond three generations. A hard-working man in shirt sleeves and his wife build a business, perhaps they operate a factory. He works constantly because times are hard and he must provide for his family. His wife does not care if the man is not always understanding. She is grateful that he works so hard.

These people are symbolic of a generation. By applying discipline, commitment, long hours and hard labor, they achieve success while raising their children, the second generation, with a reasonable work ethic. The problem is that as the first generation, they eventually make some effort to enjoy the fruits of their labor. The children, who have contributed little and have failed to learn from experience encountered by their parents, also enjoy the benefits. In fact, they gradually take the benefits for granted. The son does not work as hard as the father. He is further removed from the factory floor. Perhaps he benefits from having a college education or an MBA.

The son of the founder has children, but they are far removed from the sacrifice and effort made by their grandfather. They lack the tools or work ethic to retain their elders' road to success. Untethered by their prior generation, they will either, on their own or by hiring unqualified managers, instill decisions that jeopardize the business.

My family is a model of the last three generations of American military if the pattern holds. My father, Colonel Richard Evans, was a military leader and as a civilian devoted his life to the protection of his country. His son, the SAC Brat, devoted one year of active duty during six years of reserves to his country's defense. His son has not had to devote a day to the defense of his nation. This pattern is due to the success of Richard Evans' generation in securing his nation's power for several generations. The result was a temporarily reduced need for me and my son to defend our nation. A business that reaches great success due to the founder's great effort and success can operate for several generations due to the momentum of the founder.

Does successful military momentum due to the efforts of Colonel Evans' generation mean war between the major powers will be avoided? The concept of "shirt sleeve to shirt sleeve in three generations" would argue that the danger is greater that the nation will witness both an economic and military reversal as challenging as the 1930s Great Depression and World War II. Thus "shirt sleeve to shirt sleeve in three generations." The Kondratieff Wave does not seem to address these phenomena, but I think it is a portion of what drives the cycle.

In summary, at the conclusion of a Kondratieff depression, much of the debt is forgiven via default causing high unemployment. New technology vastly increases future production and unemployment, and the people suffer from the transitional chaos. This suffering puts the nation back into "shirt sleeves" and creates a hard-working class of people. These three systems in their pain and destruction reinvigorate the economy for another cycle. There is little debt, new technology and a lean and mean working population to push the economy for decades. This cycle is almost biological and why not, so are we.

Each nation, depending on geography, resources and other factors, concludes the down wave with a change in their relative power. This likely makes the "trough war" necessary to sort this out and set the "New Order."

The leadership of the Strategic Air Command understood how complacency can creep into any organization. In some ways, the more successful the organization the greater the vulnerability. Unfortunately, there is only so much that can be done. Decades after Pax American was created by SAC leaders, our military appears bloated with the tip of the spear greatly reduced. This can be seen by the huge increase in the per capita number of General Officers today versus the Cold War years. It is also noticeable that our nation's citizens are less interested in accepting the responsibility of serving in the military, let alone allow a functioning selective service system whereby have an unwillingness to do military service and have a draft. Is this situation a strong indication of moral decay or is it a function of many years of safety in the Continental United States communicating a lack of danger and thus no need to stand up and serve? I think cyclic events will change this situation and out of extreme crisis America will rise to the challenge. She always has.

My father, Colonel Evans, was a student of history. He respected and understood that experience in any positive endeavor in life increases one's success. At SAC, the repetitive training enabled the airmen and pilots to fulfill their jobs as a second nature. History is simply an extension of that experience often beyond our lives.

When I started my career in the financial arena, I decided to learn the history of the American Stock Market. I spent many hours studying the microfilm or stacks of the *Wall Street Journal* at the Los Angeles County Library. I began to observe and analyze. I was able to look at a Dow Jones chart in April 1898 and then attempt to predict what would happen. Instead of having to wait a few years via the tough teacher called "experience", I was able to scroll the microfilm forward to perceive a closely accurate outcome.

I want to share a few cardinal observations. Markets, as measured by the Dow Jones Industrial Average move in five waves or three advances. Importantly, the result was the greatest movement in the other direction upon completion. I eventually shared this observation with an older friend in the business and he said, "Why you are talking about Elliott Wave."

I learned that there was an entire theory about markets which concluded that market patterns as seen in a chart are fractal, have predictive qualities and operate within the dynamics of the Fibonacci ratio. I learned how to use this tool initially from the works of market analyst Edson Gould and later the extensive writings of Robert Prechter. Prechter elevated Elliott Wave to an unmatched level.

The theory unlocks markets for millions of people making independent free will choices, yet the market as presented in averages or totality, patterns. The pattern's predictive message and the success in the resulting price action implies a predestination or destiny. To quote Bob Prechter the markets provide evidence of "herding behavior in humans." Perhaps the ancient Greeks, Presbyterian and Nicholas Kondratieff had things right.

It is difficult to defend an argument asserting that cycles are sustained for more than a generation when there is insufficient data for an adequate timeline. You are dead before you can complete the test. Small fractals or patterns in stock or other liquid markets provide a laboratory to properly disprove the theory. Repeatedly being able to correctly call future market movement based on three-to-six-week, six-month and multi-year structures over time periods makes a powerful argument that decade long fractals are in play and ruled by the same laws of herding and thus a predestination resulting from the free will decisions of market players.

The analogy would be if a student learned that dropping a coin resulted in a force pulling the coin to the ground. One might try dropping a bag of coins to see if the same force was in play. After two successes, the investigator might be willing to bet that if he drops a bag of cement over a railing it will fall to the ground. It does not take a genius to decide that maybe driving a car off a cliff is unnecessary to prove a force pulls objects toward the earth. The progression of smaller to larger items tested represents larger fractals. In the case of markets, the fractals are measured in time. If there is a predictive force in play concerning market direction in each larger fractal of time, assumption can be made of multi-year structures that are near complete and their implications for the economy. For example, a five-year structure implying the largest decline of the structure in stocks likely would predict a recession since stocks precede the economy and recession correlate with stock market declines.

At this point you are likely to think, "what does this have to do with economic theory or even the name of this book?" This book is focused on the military life of Colonel Evans and of his SAC Brats son and family and their lives in a special time in history. Economics creates the struggle that brings on war and history. Markets predict economics. Correct market analysis provides insight into future events as being interpreted as positive or negative. If a future interpretation that has a positive correlation of predicting market behavior follows the same forces can predict economic events as a positive or negative. If during a recession market indicators predict a large market advance, the market is predicting good news for the economy. The reverse is also true. This is not a random or free will observation. It is cyclic and powerful

The fascinating aspect of Elliott Wave is that it not only has predictive qualities concerning future market prices but in making these predictions it provides insight into future economic and even military activities. For example, Wave analysis predicted the 1962 market crash. The completion of the pattern was in October of 1962 which indicated a market bottom was being formed and thus good news in the future. This signal was a week or so before the settlement of the Cuban missile crisis.

This theory set up a buy signal thus projecting good news a week or so prior to Lyndon Johnson's 1968 statement that he would not run again for president. A buy signal was set up weeks prior to President Nixon's decision to take the United State off the gold standard in international settlements in 1971. Attempts to analyze what the market would do if one knew in advance Nixon's move were problematic. The buy signal told us that the interpretation would be viewed in a positive light. Many will consider these views nonsense, but those educated in the works of R. N. Elliott will understand what I mean.

In 1987, the market was completing a three-year fractal. We were so confident of a severe market decline based on technical readings and on data analysis of the Elliott Wave that I ran ads in *Investors' Business Daily* warning people and telling them that we were "100% in Treasury Bills". These ads were placed in September 1987. The consequence was the 1987 market crash. In December 1987 after the "crash," we ran ads stating, "We are 100% long in the stock market, why isn't your advisor?" My firm did not place ads prior to or after 1987. One of the results of that success and our track record was that FX 500 Ltd according to *Managed Account Reports* was the largest Commodity Trading Advisor in the United States specializing in the stock index futures. At one point, we were larger than the next three firms combined. My firm's name in 1987 was Evans, Brinkerhoff and Nelson, Inc. and changed to FX 500 Ltd.

In June 1990 our indicators along with our Elliott Wave interpretation gave a sell signal. My firm went net short the market. Saddam Hussein invaded Kuwait weeks later as the market fell over 20 percent. A buy signal was generated weeks prior to the successful Operation Desert Storm freeing Kuwait.

There are many examples of news following the signals and the market. What makes this methodology so interesting is that it behaves like an animal. It adheres to nature. The main example is the tendency of the market to trade around the Fibonacci ratio of .6187 and .3813. Another example is the fractal behavior. Both characteristics are extensive in nature. It is as if the masses of humanity in their herding behavior in markets are part of a larger entity almost as if the individuals were a cell in a larger predictable organism.

The market is an excellent testing ground for predestination and free will. The market is made up of millions of humans on their own or via an advisor making free will decisions and thus we should have random price movement. If price movement is predictive by patterning and cycles, then isn't it "predestined?" I think that we have not figured out the connection between cyclic behavior in history, the economy and markets but it is far from random and more likely explainable via animal spirits and emotion and not logic. As the lead character in the movie *The Big Short* stated there are "markers." These are simply historic events that regularly proceeded with the expected result learned by experience or more likely by studying history.

This portion of the book is not an infomercial to hype me as a money manager. I do not want clients and I do not have any clients having retired in 1998. My purpose is to share what I think are useful ideas related to markets, the economy, war and the future of our nation. These views may be wrong but my take on history indicates there is a positive correlation between markets, economies and war. Advantage is gained in the event a portion of these forces have high predictive correlations. I do not pretend to have the answers but seek the truth like any other person.

At this point you may have concluded that I should have named this book "SAC Bat." I know to some trained to view people as logical, my viewpoints are Batty. Please bear with me.

"Tuna Theory" is the proposition that when wealth becomes too polarized or concentrated in too few hands the economy will fail. The greatest United States depression occurred likely under Andrew Jackson during the 1837-1848s time period. This was a time in which President Jackson removed the treasury gold from the Bank of the United States and the bank was forced to close. Banks all over the country folded. There is limited information concerning this debacle in terms of concentration of wealth. The actions by Jackson were in response to an overleveraged vulnerable economy with massive land speculation, one of the contributors.

The 1930s Great Depression was the second worse business contraction in our history and there is considerable evidence of a concentration of wealth being an important factor in the collapse. There may be an excellent explanation for why the concentration of wealth would contribute to the business debacle, but I have never read a good explanation.

Tuna Theory attempts to explain why polarization of wealth would predate a collapse. This is important because our nation is polarized by extreme wealth in the hands of the top 1 percent of the population.

SAC Brat and son Saxon "Rowdy" investigating tuna theory

"Tuna Theory" provides an attempt to answer!

In the ocean the basis of life is trillions of plankton, a combination of plant and animal deriving energy from the sun. Sardines number in the billions as baitfish that feed on the plankton. Tuna are available in the millions, feeding on sardines. Plankton is analogous to the economy's middle to lower economic class. Sardines correspond to the middle to upper class. Tuna are the top one percent apex predators. In our economy, the relationship represents a pyramid with the greatest number of people in the lower middle to lower economic class. A moderate number represents the upper middle class and obviously, a miniscule number defines the few in the top one percent. What happens if the plankton are weakened? Sardines exploit the weakness and multiply. It is easier for the sardines to take advantage of the weakened plankton. How do the tuna react? They prosper because of the increase in the population of sardines. The tuna feed on the sardines and increase in numbers. The plankton are like the economy's middle to lower economic class in the economy. The sardines are the middle to upper class, and the tuna are the top 1 percent.

If the lower class is financially weakened, they will work for less income to make ends meet. The upper middle class gain some advantage due to the resulting lower costs in their businesses. It is interesting that from limited records commodity producers, labor unions, and farmers tend to do poorly a few years prior to a collapse. Those sectors are often low paying yet a major cost of business.

What happens if the plankton begins to expire? Sardines are weakening from insufficient food sources. The tuna continues to prosper since sardine numbers have not collapsed but are weakened and thus easier to take advantage of.

The termination process in our economy would refer to small earners going bankrupt. In our economy, when numerous small businesses become less competitive, larger companies and real estate buyers temporarily benefit. The better capitalized players can snatch relative bargains at the expense of lower income earners. Note how the top one percent could capitalize on the Great Recession buying thousands of distressed homes.

Periodic recessions help the ultra-rich highest one percent because they are the most likely to have access to capital. They take advantage of the bargains a recession provides, furnished at the expense of the lower economic classes. The problem occurs when the bargains have no buyers in the decimated lower classes to buy at higher prices. The final phase occurs as the plankton and sardines are dying (bankruptcy) in large numbers. The tuna torment as their food supply collapses.

In the economy the weakest financial players naturally show the first signs of problems. The wealth of the upper 1 percent is maintained by a lower and middle class that can buy, finance and work for production. These two classes must be financially stable enough to purchase production and pay the rent, which is the ultimate basis of stock and real estate valuations. If this process fails, it resembles the strategic breakdown of a biological system.

A collapse in the underlying sectors will bring down the top one percent. In historic debt default, sectors will also bring down the top 1 percent. In extreme debt defaults in history even kings become penniless or worse lose their lives. This is why cyclically the upper one percent is successful at the expense of the other 99 percent until all sectors are decimated. Again, like Elliott Wave, the economy appears to reflect a biological system and less, the characteristics of a machine.

In the event the world experiences a great Depression, government will drastically raise tax rates in an attempt to help the recovery of the lower economic classes and reduce the polarization of wealth. The markets will have done this job for them. It will just be another example of the government closing the barn door gate after the stallion got to the mares.

I was blessed as a young person to grow up among such brave men during the Cold War. I am beyond thankful for their sacrifice and their example. If you are a SAC Brat or any military Brat, you are a member of a special group. We did not earn the right to be in this fraternity. Our parents paid the price of our entry. That price was often premature death or divorce.

I have written about emotion versus intellect in human decision making. A liberal will likely argue that we must use our compassion to move forward and that is a valid viewpoint. A conservative would likely focus on the animal in us or human nature. Their view would likely be that there is nothing new under the sun and we must temper our emotions with lessons learned from history. As a cohort, we will make many of the same mistakes our ancestors made. At the extreme perhaps a true republican is short term-cruel, but long-term kind, and a democrat is short term kind and long-term cruel, but this narrow definition attempting to shoehorn an entire population is a stretch at best.

If long waves of almost a biological nature drive history, then what control does a leader have? He or she becomes a leader because they offer the herd something the herd accepts and will follow. Is the leader in control? If history is pre-ordained or destined, what is the point of the individual participating in the great struggles facing each of our times except for figuring out the game, surviving in the greatest comfort, and raising one's children?

There is a scene in the movie *Gone with the Wind* in which the logical and cynical Rhett Butler decides to join and fight for the Confederacy. Butler is not a man defending slavery or states' rights. Butler is a man that seems to believe in nothing except himself. From the beginning of the Civil War, he has logically predicted the South's defeat. He views the men that have joined the Confederate Army to fight as fools. Now after four years of war, the South is facing certain defeat, but Butler joins the fight. The most logical of the men became illogical.

Call it patriotism or characterize it as nationalism. It is undeniably a powerful force. Perhaps in a nation of people sharing common language and genes it is a force that perpetuates one's genes, that is, what we hold in common. It is a bond based on where we are born and the people with whom we identify. It frames the motivation that causes men willing to fight for "my country right or wrong." I am not arguing that this is always moral, but I think it is a genuine force. An individual cannot change the tide of history. Can one individual prevent the eventual challenge and indigenous threat that China presents to the United States.?

The individual can have free will in personal decision making. Perhaps his actions will influence a close contest so that he prevails or even triumphs. Is this any different than a pack of wolves defeating another pack attempting to secure hunting rights? Isn't this pattern likely present to pass on the winners' genes or in the human realm, ideas into the future? In a sense it is what the ultimate portrayal of patriotism is. Is this why people have a stronger bond with people that share the greatest number of characteristics are the most compatible? In choosing a mate via computer dating aren't the questions designed to resolve what the parties have in common with the knowledge that this will lead to greater marital success? Don't we generally gravitate to the opposite sex with whom we have the most in common? The rules of the contest are predestined, and unavoidable. Did the Americanization policies of the 19th and mid-20th century tend to unite our nation? Do the "do your own thing" and "diversity is strength" arguments unite a people and make their country stronger?

After World War II there were two systems competing for World Dominance. Democracy is a system of government where power is held by the people through free elections and individual rights are protected, while communism is an ideology aiming for a classless, stateless society with collective ownership, though in practice, due to human nature, it has resulted in totalitarian, one-party states. Democracy typically features capitists economies and personal freedom, while communist states centrally plan the economy, restricting private property and individual choice.

The men of SAC could not avoid the contest between the Soviet Union and the United States, for it was likely driven by the biological forces of history, cycles, and the crowd. Forces beyond a man's control. These patriots used their free will to win that contest. Perhaps their free will determined the non-nuclear level of conflict needed to decide which system would prevail. One would argue that men like Harry Truman, Dwight Eisenhower, John Kennedy, Ronald Reagan and Curtis LeMay performed an extraordinary job of containing the Cold War below the nuclear threshold while freezing geographic boundaries of the Iron Curtain. In this context, it is not possible to dismiss the matchless role played by the dedicated patriots, whose "profession was peace," and who positioned themselves front and center, presenting the iron fist covered by the velvet glove, nor is it possible to dismiss their wives and SAC Brats who hugged them as they returned from their arduous mission defending mankind.

Is there good and evil in the cycles of history? Does good always win in the end? I guess that depends on when you arbitrarily choose to determine the end and which side you are on.

My father Colonel Richard "Eager" Evans said it a different way to me. "Perhaps we are just a bunch of ants floating down the Tennessee River with all of us yelling I am steering I am steering."

Student pilot, age 19

Final flight, age 80

Bibliography

Selected background sources for the major people, institutions, and events referenced in this book.

Balfour Declaration, 2 November 1917. Avalon Project / UK National Archives.

Beckman, Robert. *Supertiming.*

Beckman, Robert. *The Downwave.*

Berg, A. Scott. *Lindbergh.*

Braudel, Fernand. *Civilization and Capitalism, 15th–18th Century.*

Buchanan, Patrick. *Churchill, Hitler and the Unnecessary War.*

Budiansky, Stephen. *Air Power: The Men, Machines, and Ideas That Revolutionized War, from Kitty Hawk to Iraq.*

Coffey, Thomas. *Iron Eagle.*

Cipolla, Carlo M. *Guns, Sails and Empires: Technological Innovation and the Early Phases of European Expansion, 1400–1700.*

Dallek, Robert. *Franklin D. Roosevelt and American Foreign Policy.*

D'Este, Carlo. *Patton A Genius for War.*

Fernández-Armesto, Felipe. *Pathfinders: A Global History of Exploration.*

Fromkin, David. *A Peace to End All Peace.*

Herzl, Theodor. *The Jewish State.*

Hobsbawm, Eric. *The Age of Empire, 1875–1914.*

Howard, Michael. *The First World War.*

Imperial War Museums. Background essays on Dunkirk, Mers-el-Kébir, and the Battle of Britain.

Irving, David. *Churchill's War Triumph in Adversity.*

Keegan, John. *The Second World War.*

Kennedy, Paul. *The Rise and Fall of the Great Powers.*

Kershaw, Ian. *Hitler.*

Kissinger, Henry. *Metternich, Castlereagh and the Problem of Peace.*

Koskoff, David. *Joseph Kennedy A Life and Times.*

Macgregor, Douglas. *Margin of Victory.*

MacMillan, Margaret. *Paris 1919: Six Months That Changed the World.*

Mahan, Alfred Thayer. *The Influence of Sea Power upon History, 1660–1783.*

Mearsheimer, John. *The Israel Lobby and US Foreign Policy.*

Michener, James. *Poland.*

Mises, Ludwig von. *The Theory of Money and Credit.*

National Museum of the United States Air Force. Materials on the B-17 Flying Fortress, Strategic Air Command, and Offutt Air Force Base.

Official histories and archival materials for Offutt Air Force Base and Strategic Air Command.

Paret, Peter. *Clausewitz and the State.*

Parry, J. H. *The Age of Reconnaissance.*

Prechter, Robert. *The Elliott Wave Principle.*

Shirer, William L. *The Rise and Fall of the Third Reich.*

Smithsonian National Air and Space Museum. Materials on Billy Mitchell and strategic bombing.

Steiner, Zara. *The Lights That Failed: European International History, 1919–1933.*

Tucker, Robert. *Stalin in Power.*

U.S. Air Force Historical Research Agency. Materials on Strategic Air Command and Curtis E. LeMay.

Weinberg, Gerhard L. *A World at Arms.*

www.ingramcontent.com/pod-product-compliance
Lightning Source LLC
LaVergne TN
LVHW100314210926
848480LV00003B/1111